How to SEW

With over 80 Techniques and 20 Easy Projects

COLLINS & BROWN

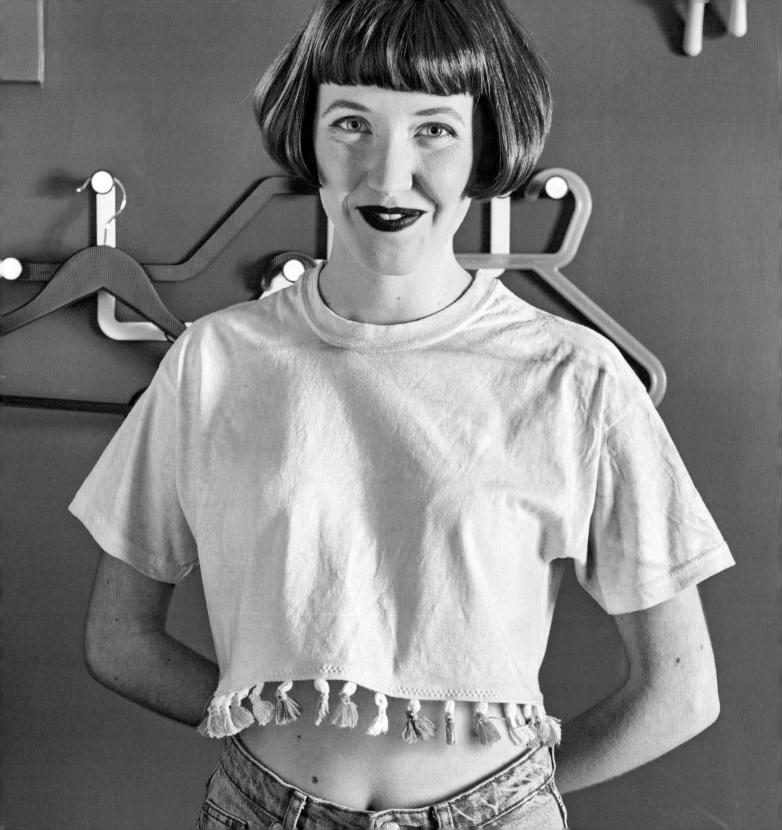

Contents

INTRODUCTION   4

PROJECTS

Wedding charms   6

Fancy fabric flowers   10

Tassel-fringed kimono top   14

Bird-shaped cushion   18

Bird appliqué peg bag   21

Shrews in a shoe   24

Easy peasy patchwork quilt   30

True love cushions   34

Make-up brush roll   38

Hedgehog sewing set   42

Trapeze sundress   46

Take three tees   53

Badger pillow   58

Trimmed Christmas stocking   61

Dapper bear pyjama case   64

Foxy sleep mask   69

Fruity floor cushions   72

Hot water bottle covers   77

Photo album cover   80

Button-up A-line skirt   84

TECHNIQUES

Sewing equipment   92

Stitching by hand   97

Using a sewing machine   105

Working with fabric   114

Seams and hems   118

Zips and buttons   130

Trimming and binding   134

Machine embellishing   141

A few tips for making clothes   144

TEMPLATES   148

INDEX   159

Get stitching!

I'm always excited by the endless possibilities presented by an uncut length of beautiful fabric. It's that sense of it just waiting to be transformed into something unique with some clever cutting and stitching. Whether you're making a wardrobe update, a project for the home, or a handcrafted gift for family and friends, nothing beats that feeling of creating something from just a few pieces of material.

This crafty collection features 20 easy projects to help you start sewing, whatever your level of experience. From a summer dress and a pattern-free kimono to a snuggly quilt and his and hers hot water bottle covers, there's plenty to inspire you for every season.

Sewing's one of the crafts I'm still a beginner at, so I'll be learning along with you. With over 80 techniques explained and demonstrated in these makes, we'll soon be working those sewing machines like a pro!

Cath

Cath Dean
Editor, *Mollie Makes*

Projects

Wedding charms

These traditional good luck charms make super little presents for a bride and her bridesmaids, and they are an excellent way to practise some all important hand stitches, including backstitch and blanket stitch. But these motifs aren't strictly weddings only! You could easily use them to create felt toys by scaling up the templates.

MATERIALS

Felt: dark grey, light grey, baby pink, candy pink, white and pistachio green

Embroidery or sewing threads in shades to match felt colours

Small amount of polyester stuffing

1cm (⅜in) wide satin ribbon in shades to match your felt colours

Pins and small, sharp scissors

Sharp embroidery needle

SIZE

Cake: 6 x 8cm (2⅜ x 3⅛in)
Turtle: 7.5 x 9cm (3 x 3½in)
Cat: 8 x 9.5cm (3⅛ x 3¾in)
Horseshoe: 8 x 8cm (3⅛ x 3⅛in)

FEATURED TECHNIQUES

- Stitching by hand: backstitch [p. 98]; blanket stitch [p. 103]; French knots [p. 104]

BEFORE YOU BEGIN

Felt is a great place to start your sewing adventures as the edges of the fabric do not fray when cut. Use a medium-density felt for this project – you could change the colours of the charms to match your wedding colour scheme.

If you don't have any polyester stuffing, cotton wool will work just as well.

Sewing Story

It is a tradition to give the bride a token to hold on her wedding day, to wish her well and to bestow her with good luck. Different cultures have different good luck symbols – for example, in China, a turtle represents wealth, longevity and good health – and I've included three more designs for you to choose from. *Charlie Moorby*

 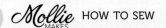

METHOD

{01} Cut your backing pieces

Start by cutting out two identical backing shapes for the base of each of the charms using the templates provided on p. 148. The backing shape is the outer outline on each of the templates and these should be cut from a contrasting felt colour so that the appliqué really stands out: candy pink has been used for the cat, dark grey for the turtle, and white for the cake and horseshoe.

{02} Cut the appliqué pieces

Using the templates provided (see p. 148) and the finished project photograph on p. 7 to guide you, cut out all the other pieces of felt that you will need to complete each charm appliqué. Use small sharp scissors to cut the intricate pieces as neatly as possible.

{03} Layer and stitch the details onto the appliqué pieces

Now begin layering and stitching the small details onto the appliqué pieces, such as the ears, eyes and nose onto the cat's head, and the belly and heart onto the cat's body. Use thread to match the felt piece being sewn on, working small backstitches with a sharp embroidery needle. Sew on very small pieces, like the cat's pupils, with tiny cross stitches.

{01}

{02}

{03}

{04}

{04} Join the appliqué pieces to a backing shape

Pin and stitch the appliqué pieces onto one of the backing shapes for your chosen charm. Start stitching around the edge of the appliqué pieces to secure them in place, working your backstitches close to the edge to mirror the outline of the design. Add any additional stitched details such as the small stitch beneath the cat's nose for the mouth, for example, and the progressively longer stitches at either side of the nose for the whiskers.

Note

Small appliqué details, such as the cat's and turtle's eyes and the flower centres, are held in place with tiny cross stitches, but you could use French knots if you prefer.

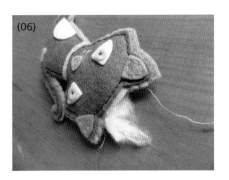

{06}

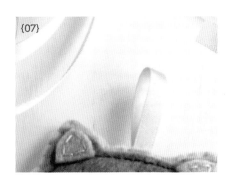

{07}

{05} Join the front and back

Once all the stitching on the front piece is complete, pin it to the remaining backing piece, taking care to line up the pieces as neatly as possible. Blanket stitch around the edge of the charm, leaving a gap for stuffing at the top of the design.

{06} Fill with stuffing

Gently fill the charm with a little polyester stuffing (or cotton wool) but do not overstuff it, as the stuffing may become visible through the blanket stitch edge.

{07} Make the hanging loop

Make a small hanging loop from a short length of ribbon, slip it into the stuffing gap and stitch the opening closed. For the horseshoe charm, both of the top edges are left open for stuffing, and a longer length of ribbon is inserted into each opening to make a handle for carrying.

CHARLIE MOORBY
AKA THE SAVVY CRAFTER

Charlie is a thrifty craft blogger and incurable stitching addict with a penchant for anything handmade. Commissioning Editor by day and crafter by night, you'll find her collecting buttons and hoarding ribbons on a daily basis. She's a dab hand with a pencil and loves a spot of cross stitching too. Find her online at www.thesavvycrafter.co.uk.

Note

When joining the front and back pieces at step 5, you could add extra lengths of ribbon to the bottom edge of the charms to add an extra celebratory touch, as seen on the turtle.

Fancy fabric flowers

Become a fabric florist and fill your home with an everlasting array of beautiful buds and blooms made from floral prints. They'll make a wonderful table centrepiece displayed in vintage cups, or you can pin them to dresses, coats and hats. They are also a great way to explore one of your sewing essentials – fusible webbing.

MATERIALS

Toning small-print fabrics of your choice

Sewing threads to match

Double-sided fusible webbing

Stiff wire for flower stems

Decorative craft wire for leaf stems

Ribbon

Iron

Sewing needle

Pinking shears, dressmaker's scissors and scissors for cutting wire

FEATURED TECHNIQUES

- Cutting fabric on the bias [p. 117]
- Stitching by hand: running stitch [p. 98]

BEFORE YOU BEGIN

To make the flower for each bloom or bud, you will need two small-print floral fabrics in the same colour tone each approximately 35cm (14in) square, as well as a little green fabric for the leaves.

Use a decorative craft wire for the leaf stems, such as DMC Color Infusions Memory Thread, which is a soft fibre-wrapped wire that can be couched in place with a co-ordinating sewing thread.

Cutting on the bias gives the petal shapes a little bit of stretch for a lovely curvy look.

JENNY DIXON

A craft journalist by trade, Jenny has always loved to make things. She is based in Bath in the UK, where she shares her home with an outrageously large fabric stash. Find her online at: jennysbuttonjar.wordpress.com.

Sewing Story

I love the vintage style of the fabric flowers I have created, and as far as blooms go, I think the bigger the better. So, to make an even more flamboyant bloom, you could add an extra row of large petals – you'll need an additional 11 petals for this. *Jenny Dixon*

{02}

METHOD: BLOOM

{01} Prepare your fabric pieces

Taking two fabrics of your choice, use fusible webbing to fuse them together with wrong sides facing. Use the petal templates (p. 150) to cut seven small petals and eight large petals on the bias by placing templates diagonally on the fabric. Cut a 2 x 30cm (¾ x 12in) fabric strip also on the bias. Snip into the centre of each petal as marked with a dotted line on the templates.

Gently fray the edges of the petals by using a pin to pull some of the threads free. Concentrate on the top edge of the petal, as this will show most. Screw the petal up into a tight ball and roll it between your fingers. Open out, hold the corners and tug. Repeat for all petals and along one long edge of the fabric strip.

{02} Make the flower centre

Take the fabric strip and roll one end to give you a tight start, then work outwards, coiling and twisting the fabric as you go, and keep holding it tight so that it can't uncurl. When you reach the end of the strip, tuck the loose end underneath and secure with a few stitches, adding a few stitches to the back of the coil too, to keep it in place.

{03} Add the small petals

Starting with the smaller petals first, overlap the slit fabric at the petal base for a curved shape and stitch to the back of the flower centre. Add the next petal slightly overlapping the first, repeating to add all the small petals.

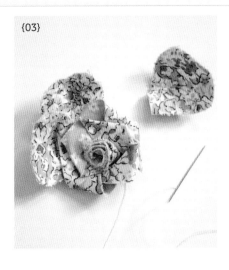

{03}

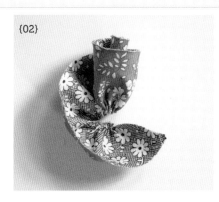

{02}

{04}

METHOD: BUD

{01} Prepare and cut out the fabric pieces
Take two fabrics and fuse them together with wrong sides facing using fusible webbing. Cut a 4 x 30cm (1½ x 12in) fabric strip on the bias as well as five small petals (templates, p. 150) also on the bias.

{02} Make the flower centre
Gather the fabric strip: work small running stitches along one edge and pull tight. Start by rolling the strip tightly, then a little more loosely, until you reach the end; stitch through the base of the coil to secure.

{03} Add the petals
Add each of the large petals in turn around the flower centre: keep them close and upright and overlap them as you go. To give a more realistic look, roll the top edge of the petals and crease with your fingernail to hold it in place.

{04} Make the stem
Cut a piece of stiff wire for the stem and push it into the base. Cut a 4cm (1½in) fabric circle and make a snip to the centre. Fit the fabric circle around the stem and fold it into a cone shape to fit neatly around the base of the flower, then stitch it in place.

{04} Add the large petals
Attach the outer row of eight large petals in the same way as the small petals (see step 3).

{05} Finish the flower
Use pinking shears to cut a small circle of your chosen fabric and sew it over the back of the flower for strength; fix a safety pin to the fabric circle so that the finished flower can be easily attached to an outfit .

{06} Make the leaves
Use pinking shears to cut two large leaves from green fabric; fold in half and press the 'vein' lines. Snip into the centre at the base as marked by the dotted line on the template, overlap the cut edges and attach to the flower back.

{05} Make the leaf spray
Use pinking shears to cut three small leaves from bonded fabrics. Take a length of decorative craft wire, double it and then twist it along its length. Stitch the wire to the front of one of the leaves to make a central vein and stem, couching it in place with small straight stitches. Make two more leaf stems, then twist them together to create the spray. Place the spray behind the flower stem; tightly bind stems together with ribbon, stitching the end to fasten.

Tassel-fringed kimono top

This elegant kimono top is a great way to create a garment without having to get to grips with a pattern, making it ideal for beginner sewers. The simple shape is made by cutting a few rectangles from your chosen fabric and sewing them together with basic straight stitch, then adding a tassel trim to the hem for a touch of chic.

MATERIALS

150cm (60in) of 140cm (55in) wide fabric and thread to match

2m (2⅛yd) tassel fringing

Dressmaker's scissors

Tape measure and pins

Iron

Sewing machine

SIZE

Custom fit to your measurements.

FEATURED TECHNIQUES

- Machine-stitching techniques [p. 110]
- Plain straight seam (p. 119)
- Seam finishes (p. 122)
- Machine-stitched hem (p. 125)
- Attaching fringe trims (p. 134)

BEFORE YOU BEGIN

To make sure your finished kimono hangs well, pick a fabric with good drape, such as viscose or silk. Hannah and Rosie chose a 100 per cent viscose rayon called Triangles from fabric designer See You At Six.

Pre-wash your fabric to ensure it won't shrink the first time you wash the finished garment. Press your fabric before beginning the project.

Use a 1.5cm (⅝in) seam allowance throughout unless otherwise stated, and be sure to finish your seams using your preferred method for your chosen fabric. Hannah and Rosie pinked the seams on their kimono.

Sewing Story

We wanted to design a simple kimono that could be made without a pattern to encourage people to take the first step towards sewing garments. It can be a little scary when you first use a pattern but this kimono uses many of the same techniques that you'd find when working with a printed pattern, so it's a great way to learn. We love it! **Hannah and Rosie**

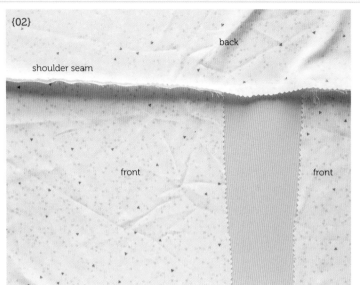

{02}

shoulder seam

back

front

front

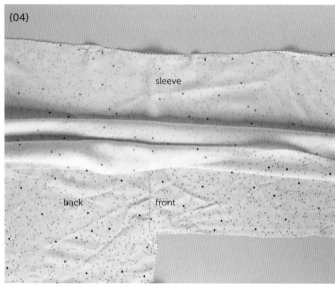

{04}

sleeve

back

front

METHOD

{01} Measure and cut the front and back fabric rectangles
Start by cutting two same-sized rectangles from your fabric to the measurements given below:
For the width: Measure from shoulder to shoulder and add 15cm (5¾in).
For the length: Measure from the top of your shoulder to halfway between your hip and knee, and add 3cm (1⅛in).

One of the rectangles you have cut will form the back of your kimono. To make the kimono front pieces, find the centre of the second rectangle, measure 5cm (2in) to each side of the centre line and cut away this area away to give you two smaller rectangles.

{02} Pin and stitch the front pieces to the back
With right sides together, pin the two front pieces to the back piece at either end of one of the short sides, matching raw edges. These will be your shoulder seams; stitch together. Finish seams and press towards the back.

{03} Measure and cut the sleeve fabric rectangles
To create the sleeves of your kimono, cut two same-sized rectangles from your fabric to the measurements given below:
For the width: Measure from the top of your shoulder to halfway between your shoulder and elbow, and add 3cm (1⅛in).

For the length: Measure from the shoulder seam to the bottom edge of the kimono then divide this number by three; now multiply this number by two and add 3cm (1⅛in).

{04} Pin and stitch the sleeve pieces to the kimono
Lay the joined back/fronts right side up; pin the sleeve rectangles to either edge of the kimono body, right sides together (the photo shows one of the sleeve rectangles being laid out along the left-hand side of the body). Match the centre of the long side of the sleeve to the shoulder seam and align the raw edges, then stitch together. Finish seams and press towards the body.

{05} Pin and stitch the sleeve and side seams

Fold your kimono at the shoulder seams, right sides together. Line up the raw edges along the underside of the sleeves and down the sides. Pin in place, then stitch together; at the underarm point where the two seams meet, you can slightly curve the seam if you wish. Snip into the seam allowance under the arm to make the fabric lie smoother around the curve (p. 121). Press seams open and finish.

{06} Cut the front/neckband piece

Cut a strip from your remaining fabric 10cm (4in) wide and at least as long as the whole of the opening at the front of your kimono – it's best to make it a little longer as it can always be trimmed later. If you need to join two pieces of fabric to give you a long enough strip, be sure to plan for the joining seam to meet at the centre back of the neck, and stitch the pieces together at one short end, with right sides facing.

{07} Stitch the front/neckband piece to the kimono

Fold your fabric strip in half lengthwise, wrong sides together, and press. Pin the strip all the way around the front opening of your kimono, with right sides together and matching up raw edges, remembering to position

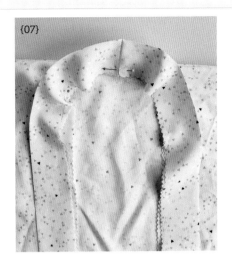

{07}

the joining seam (if you have one) at the centre back of the neck. Stitch, then clip into the curves around the neck (p. 121).

{08} Hem the sleeves

Fold under the raw edges by 1cm (⅜in), then again by 2cm (¾in). Press and pin the hem in place, then stitch carefully (these stitches will be seen, so take your time).

{09} Finish with a tassel trim hem

Turn up the bottom hem of your kimono by 1cm (⅜in), then again by 2cm (¾in), and press in place. Position your tassel trim over the pressed hem. Making sure that the tassel tape isn't poking over the edge of your hem, pin it in place, then stitch the tassel trim and hem together, this time using a zigzag stitch.

HANNAH AND ROSIE
OF THE NEW CRAFT HOUSE

Friends since childhood, Hannah and Rosie have always been obsessed with crafting. They set up The New Craft House in 2014 with the aim to encourage as many people as possible to learn new crafts. Their projects and range of craft kits all use traditional techniques in modern and stylish designs. You can find them at www.thenewcrafthouse.com and on instagram @newcrafthouse.

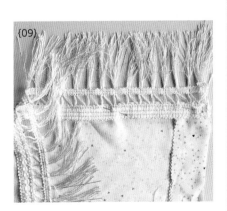

{09}

Bird-shaped cushion

This project is a great way to give new life to favourite retro-print fabrics. Using basic machine and hand-sewing techniques, you can create your very own birdie to keep you company as you craft. This chick is made from a vintage cotton fabric with wings of felt in co-ordinating colours.

MATERIALS

Two pieces of printed fabric 30 x 35cm (12 x 14in)

One piece of felt 15 x 20cm (6 x 8in) in each of two colours to co-ordinate with the printed fabric

Stranded cotton (floss) to co-ordinate with the printed fabric and felt colours

100g (4oz) polyester toy stuffing

Water-erasable fabric pen

Scissors

Iron

Sewing needle and pins

Sewing machine

Knitting needle or other blunt tool

SIZE

Approx 28cm (11in) wide by 33cm (13in) high

FEATURED TECHNIQUES

- Transferring embroidery designs [p. 100]
- Stitching by hand: running stitch [p. 98]; backstitch [p. 98]; whipstitch [p. 98]
- Machine-stitching techniques [p. 110]
- Curved seams (p. 121)
- Trimming to neaten seams [p. 119]

CLARE NICOLSON

Clare founded her interior textiles and accessories line in 2004. A lover and collector of all things vintage, she has an ever-expanding fabric collection. Clare is always creating, whether for a new collection or just for fun, and she's never far away from her sewing machine. Find her online at www.clarenicolson.com.

METHOD

{01} Cut out felt and fabric pieces

Use the templates (p. 149) to cut out two bird shapes from your fabric (making sure one is reversed) and six teardrop shapes for the wings from felt (two in one colour and four in the other colour).

{02} Sew the wings to the fabric pieces

Pin the wings into position on each of the fabric pieces. Using two strands of embroidery thread and running stitch, sew on the wings.

{03} Embroider the bird's eyes

Trace the eyes onto the right side of each bird shape using a water-erasable pen. Use three strands of embroidery thread and backstitch to stitch the eyes. Once finished, gently dab with a damp cloth to remove the pen marks.

{04} Join the front and back pieces

Align the bird pieces right sides together, and pin. Machine stitch using a 1cm (⅜in) seam allowance, leaving a 10cm (4in) gap at the bottom. Diagonally trim the corners at the beak and the tail, taking care not to cut too close to the stitching.

{05} Fill with stuffing

Turn your bird the right way out through the opening, and use a knitting needle or other blunt-pointed tool to push out the corners. Be careful not to poke through the fabric.

Fill your bird with polyester stuffing until even and plump. Pay special attention to the beak and tail, pushing stuffing into the corners. Fold over the edges of the opening and sew closed with whipstitch. To finish, give the cushion a light press on a medium heat.

{02}

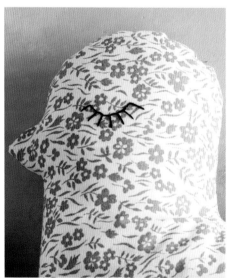

Sewing Story

I love collecting vintage fabrics and devising projects to use them up. If you don't have enough fabric to make the bird from your favourite retro-fabric, you can scale this project down to make a bird-shaped lavender sachet instead. Simply use the bird template at actual size, and for a sweet-smelling gift, fill it with a handful of dried lavender instead of stuffing. **Clare Nicolson**

Bird appliqué peg bag

No more washday blues! Cheer up the humdrum task of hanging out the washing with a machine-stitched peg bag decorated with a charming embroidered design. Reminiscent of 1950s patterns, you'll love creating the swallows in simple stitches and the chance to appliqué a whole new wardrobe of miniature clothes.

MATERIALS

One piece of embroidery linen 32 x 30cm (12½ x 12in)

Two pieces of printed fabric 32 x 30cm (12½ x 12in) for back and lining

Scraps of lightweight printed cotton fabric for appliqué

Stranded cotton (floss): dark turquoise, light turquoise and dark grey

Two small buttons

Mini hanger

Double-sided fusible webbing

Iron

Embroidery transfer pen

Small embroidery hoop

Embroidery needle

Pins, sewing needle and scissors

Sewing machine

SIZE

Approx 31cm (12⅜in) wide by 29cm (11⅜in) high

FEATURED TECHNIQUES

- Using an embroidery hoop [p. 100]
- Stitching by hand: chain stitch [p. 102]
- Fused appliqué [p. 143]
- Sewing on a button [p. 133]
- Machine-stitching techniques [p. 110]

DESIGNED BY
JENNY DIXON

BEFORE YOU BEGIN

If you are using specialist embroidery linen it will not need prewashing, but do give it a good press.

Enlarge the embroidery and appliqué design on p. 155 to actual size and transfer it onto the linen fabric using one of the transfer methods described on p. 100.

METHOD

{01} Embroider the bird embroidery design

Start by stitching the lower bird, centring that part of the design in the embroidery hoop. Using two strands of embroidery thread and chain stitch, work the lower bird in dark turquoise, then reposition the fabric in the hoop to work the top bird in light turquoise. Next stitch the washing line using one strand of grey embroidery thread and chain stitch.

{02} Appliqué the clothes

To make the clothes, trace off the main shape of each clothing item to make templates for the skirt, blouse, shorts and shirt. Iron double-sided fusible webbing onto the back of your print fabric scraps and use the templates to cut out each clothing shape. Iron each shape into position.

{03} Complete the embroidery

Using one strand of dark grey embroidery thread and dainty chain stitch, work around the clothing outlines. Then work the rest of the details. Stitch lines to represent the clothes pegs and sew the two small buttons onto the blouse.

(When you have finished, you can use a damp cloth to gently dab the appliqué to remove any transfer pen marks that show through your stitching.)

{04} Cut the peg bag fabrics

Use the peg bag template (see p. 155) to cut your embroidered linen into the shape of the bag. Also, cut a lining and back from your printed fabrics and put the back to one side for now. Mark the position of the opening on the embroidered linen front.

{05} Stitch the lining to the front

Place the embroidered linen front on top of the lining fabric with right sides together, and pin. Stitch a line around the marked opening 6mm (¼in) away from it. Carefully cut through both fabric layers along the line of the opening. Fold the embroidered front of the bag through the opening and press.

{06} Stitch the front to the back

Place the lined front on top of the peg bag back, right sides together, and machine stitch all around the outer edge using a 1cm (⅜in) seam allowance and leaving a tiny gap at the top for inserting the hook of the hanger in step 7. Turn the peg bag right side out through the front opening and press.

{07} Cover the hanger and finish

Make a tiny tube of fabric by doubling over a narrow strip of the back/lining fabric and sewing along the long edge. Thread the fabric tube onto the hook of your hanger and gather the lines of stitching so that it is a little ruched. Post the hanger into the peg bag opening and push the hook out through the tiny gap left at the top.

To finish, cut a small strip of matching fabric and tie it to the base of the hook.

Note

Fabrics that are liable to shrink should be washed and ironed before you begin. Follow the manufacturer's care guidelines for laundering.

Shrews in a shoe

Three little shrews all snug in a felt shoe – what's not to love! Get ready to impress with your topstitching finesse on the lace up, and practise small-scale seam sewing for the family trio. You may even be inspired to create your own design – cats in a hat anyone?

MATERIALS

Three pieces of plain or checked fabric 22 x 16cm (8⅝ x 6¼in) for head, arms and ear

Three pieces of printed fabric 16 x 14cm (6¼ x 5½in) for body

Three pieces of printed fabric 9 x 5cm (3½ x 2in) for ear

Small scraps of printed fabric for nose

Felt: one piece 25 x 10cm (10 x 4in) for mummy shrew's dress and one piece 24 x 22cm (9½ x 8¾in) for shoe

Sewing threads to match fabrics

Stranded cotton (floss): black and red

Two mini buttons

Polyester toy stuffing

Thin cord for shoe

Sewing machine

Pins, needles, scissors, hole punch

Small, thin-handled paintbrush

Iron

SIZE

Mummy and daddy: 18cm (7in) tall
Baby: 11cm (4¼in) tall
Shoe: 22 x 9cm (8⅝ x 3½in)

FEATURED TECHNIQUES

- Machine-stitching techniques [p. 110]
- Curved seams [p. 121]
- Stitching by hand: slipstitch [p. 99]; backstitch [p. 98]; running stitch [p. 98]
- Topstitching [p. 113]

BEFORE YOU BEGIN

Use a narrow 6mm (¼in) seam allowance throughout. Accurate seam matching is very important, so if necessary use a masking tape guide to mark this seam allowance on your sewing machine (see p. 111).

If making this project for a young child, DO NOT use the buttons.

To make turning the small pieces of fabric easier, be sure to use thin cotton fabrics; avoid bulky fabrics or material that frays easily.

Take it slowly when machine stitching small fabric pieces together, especially around curved seams. On tight curves, lift the presser foot slightly and swivel the piece every couple of stitches.

CLARE YOUNGS

After working as a graphic designer and illustrator for a number of years, Clare turned to craft full time five years ago and she has not looked back since. She spends her day doing what she loves best – snipping, sewing, designing and making things. Catch up with her crafty way of life on her blog at www.clareyoungs.co.uk.

METHOD: SHREW

{01} Cut out the fabric pieces
Trace off the template pieces required for the adult shrew onto a piece of paper (see p. 154) and cut out – these are your pattern pieces.

Working first on one of the adult shrews, take the piece of plain or checked fabric for the head, arms and ear, fold in half and pin together. Pin the head, arms and ear patterns onto the fabric and cut them out to give you two heads, four arms and two ears. (You may find it easier to draw around the patterns and then remove them before cutting out.)

Take your larger piece of printed fabric, fold in half with wrong sides together and use your pattern to cut out the body pieces. From the smaller piece of folded printed fabric, cut the remaining two ears. From your scrap of printed fabric, cut two nose pieces.

{02} Pin and sew the ear pieces
Take one printed ear piece and one plain ear piece, place right sides together and pin. Sew a seam around the curved side, leaving the straight edge open. Trim the seam down to 3mm (⅛in) and cut small snips into the seam at the curve. Turn right way out. Repeat to make the second ear.

{03} Pin and sew the arm pieces
Take two arm pieces, place right sides together and pin. Sew around arm leaving the straight edge open. Trim seam to 3mm (⅛in) and turn arm right way out. Repeat to make the second arm.

{04} Pin and sew the nose pieces to the head pieces
Take one nose and one head piece, place right sides together, matching straight edge to straight edge, and pin in place. Sew across the seam and then trim seam to 3mm (⅛in). Repeat to make second joined head piece.

(05) Pin and sew the head pieces to the body pieces
Take the joined head piece and one body piece, place right sides together so top edge of body aligns with the straight edge of the head section, and pin in place. Sew a seam across and trim to 3mm (⅛in). Repeat to make second joined head/body piece.

Before continuing, press all the sewn-together pieces.

{06} Pin ears and arms in place and join body pieces together

Take one of the joined head/body pieces and place right side up on your work surface. Pin the ears in position on the head, placing them so that the pattern side faces to the front on one ear and to the back on the other. Pin the arms in position at the top of the body. Note that the ears and arms face inwards and overlap the side edge of the body by a few millimetres.

Place the second joined head/body piece on top, so that right sides are together, making sure to align edges and match seams. Pin in position, and tack together if you choose to. Sew very slowly around the edge, taking great care at the curved sections and leaving a gap approx 5cm (2in) long down one side of the shrew's body for stuffing.

Trim the seam all the way around to 3mm (⅛in), and trim off the bits of arms and ears that are sticking out. Clip into any curved section as before. Carefully turn the shrew the right way out (see note below) and press.

Note

The nose section is very thin so it takes some easing to get the fabric through – the handle of your small, thin paintbrush may be helpful here.

{07} Fill with stuffing

Use polyester toy filling to stuff the shrew: start by pushing tiny amounts of the stuffing into the nose and legs using the handle of your paintbrush to help you to get it into the small spaces; then continue to pad out the head and body, but do not overfill. At the turning gap, turn in the raw edges and use small slipstitches to sew up the side as neatly as possible.

{08} Embroider the facial details

First embroider the eye: thread a needle with three strands of the black embroidery thread; do not tie a knot at the end of the thread. Take the needle into the body of the shrew 5–6cm (2–2⅜in) away from where you want to position the eye. Bring the needle out where you want to stitch the eye, and pull the thread through until it just disappears into the body. Make three tiny stitches on top of each other, then take the needle through the head to come out at the other side. Stitch the eye on this side in the same way, then take

Note

If you don't have embroidery thread in the right colours, you could double or treble up sewing thread as you only need a tiny bit.

the needle into the body and bring it up a few centimetres away from the eye. Snip off the thread to lose the thread end within the body.

Now thread your needle with three strands of the red embroidery thread, and work the mouth in a similar way with just a couple of stitches. Your adult shrew is now complete. Repeat the whole process to make a partner.

{09} Make mummy shrew's dress

Trace off the dress template from p. 154 and cut out in paper. Use the dress pattern to cut out two dress pieces from your felt fabric. Place the dress pieces together and pin. Sew a 6mm (¼in) seam across both shoulders and up each side and underarm, then trim the seam down to 3mm (⅛in). Sew the buttons on.

{10} Adaptations for baby shrew

The baby is made in exactly the same way as the adult shrews but using different templates (see p. 154). For the closed eye, stitch a little curved line of backstitch or running stitch on either side of baby's head.

METHOD: SHOE

{01} Cut out fabric pieces
Trace off the shoe template (see p. 154) and cut out of paper. Pin the shoe pattern to the felt and cut it out. Cut out one more shoe shape from the felt: most felt does not have a wrong or a right side but if yours does, flip the pattern. Use a hole punch to make the three lace holes on each shoe piece.

{02} Mark topstitching guidelines
Take your shoe pattern and cut out the toe cap shape and the shape around the lace holes. Lay these cut out pieces down in position on the felt shoe shapes and use a pencil to draw the guidelines for the topstitching in these areas.

{03} Stitch the shoe
Choosing a thread colour to contrast with the felt colour, first topstitch over the marked guidelines on each shoe shape. Then place the two shoe shapes together and topstitch from the back heel and around the shoe, 6mm (¼in) from the edge, stopping at the bottom of the lace area and leaving the top of the shoe open.

{04} Lace the shoe
Taking a length of thin cord in a colour to match your topstitching, lace it through the lace holes and tie it in a bow to complete your shoe.

Sewing Story

I learnt to sew on a lovely old Singer sewing machine that had been handed down by my grandmother. I turned granny's fabric scraps into mini toys with whole wardrobes of mini clothes. By the time I moved into my first flat, I was ready for cushion and curtain making. It gives you an immense feeling of pride and satisfaction to finish something you have made yourself, and it can save you pots of money! ***Clare Youngs***

Easy peasy patchwork quilt

All the things you might just be lucky enough to see when trekking through the woods on a crisp autumn day inspired an easy-to-piece patchwork. This little quilt is the perfect size for snuggling under on the sofa, or for draping over a child's bed.

MATERIALS

10 fat quarters of quilters' cotton in a variety of nature-inspired prints

120cm (47in) of cotton fabric for backing

100cm (39in) of cotton fabric for binding

120cm (47in) of lightweight quilt wadding

White or ivory sewing thread

Sticky notes and pencil

Pins, sewing needle and scissors

Iron

Sewing machine

Rotary cutter, ruler and cutting mat

SIZE

Approx 90 x 110cm (35 x 43in)

FEATURED TECHNIQUES

- Plain straight seam [p. 119]
- Pressing: flat seams [p. 96]
- Topstitching [p. 113]
- Joining binding strips [p. 137]
- Continuous binding [p. 139]
- Stitching by hand: slipstitch [p. 99]

BEFORE YOU BEGIN

If working with pre-cut fabric bundles, these do not require prewashing. If you are using other fabric sources to make this project, wash each fabric colour separately in hot water to pre-shrink, then press while still damp for a smooth, crease-free finish; discard any fabrics that bleed.

Manufactured quilt wadding is sold by length from a roll or in standard cut sizes. Polyester wadding is a good choice as it is lightweight, inexpensive and available in many lofts (thicknesses). This type of wadding does not shrink, can be machine-washed and is quick to dry.

JANE HUGHES

Jane from littleteawagon is a crafter/ designer with a fondness for fabrics and sewing, doodling, and making and blogging about a crafty life. Discover more at teawagontales.blogspot.com.

METHOD

{01} Cut and lay out your fabrics

Use the rotary cutter, ruler and cutting mat to cut 30 squares of fabric – three from each fat quarter – measuring 20 x 20cm (8 x 8in). Press the cut squares.

Working on a clean floor, randomly place the squares to give you five rows across by six rows down, but avoid having the same pattern in any row. Label six sticky notes 1 to 6. Starting at the top left-hand corner, pin a number label on the first square of each row so all six rows are numbered. Carefully put each row of squares (in order) in a pile, with the numbered square at the top.

{02} Piece the quilt top

Using a 8mm (5/16in) seam allowance, begin sewing the first row of squares together. Sew the squares in the remaining five rows together to give you six rows of squares. Press seams open, then stitch the rows together one at a time, again with a 8mm (5/16in) seam allowance; press the seams. Flip the quilt top over, remove the number labels, then press.

{03} Add the wadding

Lay the wadding flat and put the pieced quilt on top, right side facing up and pin; trim excess wadding. Topstitch 2mm (3/32in) either side of all seams through both layers.

Sewing Story

A rotary cutter and cutting mat makes quick work of cutting out the fabric squares; if you don't have these items, you can make a card template and hand cut the squares using scissors.
Jane Hughes

{01}

{04} Add the backing

Place the pressed backing fabric right side down on the floor. Lay your quilt on top and smooth flat. Pin and trim to size. Machine stitch through all layers close to the edge of the quilt, making sure layers are straight as you work.

{05} Bind your quilt

To make the binding, cut five strips of fabric measuring 7.5 x 100cm (3 x 39in). Stitch the strips together at a 45-degree angle and press flat. Press one of the ends of the joined fabric strip at a 45-degree angle, then press the binding strip in half.

Attach the binding with a 8mm

(⁵⁄₁₆in) seam allowance beginning at X as shown (04a). At a corner, sew almost to the edge; reverse stitch, and fold the binding upwards; fold the binding back down, turn the quilt and continue (see p. 139 for more detail on binding a corner).

On the final side, stop 12cm (4¾in) from the X; trim binding to leave a 4cm (1½in) overlap and tuck this into the opening at the start. Continue stitching (04b).

To finish, pin the folded edge of the binding to the back of the quilt, mitring the corners neatly (see p. 139), and slipstitch the binding to the quilt backing.

Note

It may be best to choose the binding fabric when the quilt is finished, as it can be difficult to judge the effect before this. Spread out the quilt and try quite long strips of different widths of fabric along the edge to see how they might look.

{04a}

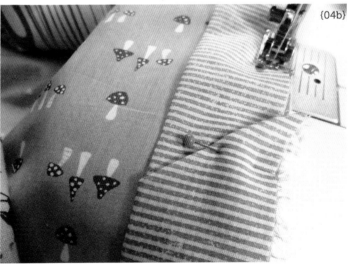

{04b}

True love cushions

The perfect Valentine's Day gift, these personalised cushions with an easy-sew envelope backing are a great way to celebrate your love all year round. Hand-stitched leather heart appliqués, inspired by 1950s rockabilly tattoos, are teamed up with cute polka-dots and an eye-catching pom-pom trim.

MATERIALS (PER PAIR)

Leather: one piece of red 20 x 20cm (8 x 8in), one piece of white 20 x 16cm (8 x 6¼in) and one piece of black 6 x 20cm (2⅜ x 8in)

1m (1⅛yd) of polka-dot fabric

3m (3¼yd) of pom-pom trim

Black embroidery thread

Two cushion pads 35 x 35cm (14 x 14in)

Fabric glue

Leather needle

Pins and scissors

Sewing machine

Iron

Tracing paper and pencil

SIZE

35 x 35cm (14 x 14in)

FEATURED TECHNIQUES

- Machine-stitching techniques [p. 110]
- Attaching in-seam trims [p. 135]
- Trimming to neaten seams [p. 119]
- For more information on working with leather, see p. 116

ZOE LARKINS

Zoe Larkins is the inspired designer-maker behind accessories label Love From Hetty & Dave, and she is most often to be found busily stitching away in her shop/studio in Bournemouth on the south coast of England. For more about her work, visit www.lovefromhettyanddave.co.uk.

BEFORE YOU BEGIN

Plan your lettering for the leather scroll appliqué in advance. Your letters should measure about 3cm (1⅛in) high. The outline of your letters need to be drawn in reverse on the suede side of the leather, so that they will read the right way round when they are cut out. You may find it helpful to write them onto tracing paper first, then flip the tracing over to copy the name onto the suede.

You may need to adjust the width of your letters to fit a longer name on the scroll. If your names are very long, you may need to use just your initials instead, or what about 'you' and 'me'?

Always use a leather needle when sewing leather – it has a triangular tip which helps the needle to glide easily through, making it so much easier to sew with.

If you find it tough on your fingertips pushing the needle through the leather, invest in a thimble. Once you get used to it, it'll save your finger and make your stitches neater.

{02}

METHOD

{01} Cut out the leather fabric
Using the templates on p. 158 and working on the suede side of the leather, cut out the heart shape from red leather, and the scroll and two scroll ends from white leather.

Cut out the letters for your names from the long strip of black leather using your tracing paper pattern to copy the names onto the suede side of the leather first (see Before You Begin for more advice on planning your lettering for the leather scroll).

{02} Assemble and stitch the leather appliqué
Use fabric glue to attach the cut out letters onto the leather side of the scroll. Using a leather needle and black embroidery thread, hand stitch the letters in place using long straight stitches, making sure that the corners in particular are securely stitched.

Now glue the scroll onto the leather side of the heart. Arrange the scroll ends and glue in place on the underside of the heart. Hand stitch all of the pieces into place with neat, straight stitches.

{03} Cut the polka-dot fabric pieces

From the polka-dot fabric, cut one piece measuring 37cm (14½in) square for the cushion front, and two rectangles measuring 20 x 37cm (8 x 14½in) and 26 x 37cm (10¼ x 14½in) for the back.

{04} Attach the appliqué and the pom-pom trim

Attach the leather heart in the centre of the polka-dot fabric square using a little glue, and hand stitch in place as before. Cut four 37cm (14½in) lengths of pom-pom trim and pin them around the edges of the fabric square, with the pom-poms facing inwards. Machine stitch the trim in place using a small zigzag stitch.

{05} Make the cushion back

Use the polka-dot fabric rectangles to make an envelope-opening cushion back. Prepare each rectangle by folding one long edge under by 6mm (¼in), then fold over again by 1cm (⅜in); press, pin and machine stitch to complete the hemming.

{06} Assemble the cushion

Lay the heart appliqué right side up on your work surface. Place the smaller hemmed rectangle on top, right side facing down, with raw edges aligning at the top and sides. Now position the larger hemmed rectangle to align the raw edges at the bottom and sides, so that it overlaps the smaller hemmed rectangle. Pin in place. Machine stitch slowly around the edges to avoid catching the pom-poms under the needle, carefully pushing them in as you sew if necessary.

Carefully snip off the corners and turn the cushion right side out. Use the point of your scissors to gently push out the corners before inserting the cushion pad.

Now make a second cushion to complete the pair.

Make-up brush roll

Keep your make-up brushes safe in this pretty fabric roll. Lined with bird-printed material, the front is decorated with a little stamped bird, wearing her pretty party crown, and a gorgeous handmade fabric ruffle. A sumptuous velvet ribbon keeps the roll in place.

MATERIALS

Natural linen: one piece 25 x 32cm (10 x 12½in) for backing and one piece 23 x 34cm (9 x 13½in) for pocket panel

Bird-printed fabric: one piece 25 x 32cm (10 x 12½in) for lining and one strip 50 x 3cm (20 x 1⅛in) for ruffle

One piece of cotton wadding 25 x 32cm (10 x 12½in)

35cm (14in) cotton lace trim

135cm (53in) velvet ribbon

Medium-weight fusible interfacing

Bird-themed rubber stamps

Black ink pad and acrylic stamp block

Pins and scissors

Ruler and pencil

Sewing machine

Iron

SIZE

Approx 30 x 23.5cm (12 x 9¼in) unrolled

FEATURED TECHNIQUES

- Straight stitch gathering [p. 135]
- Machine-stitching techniques [p. 110]
- Stitching by hand: slipstitch [p. 99]

BEFORE YOU BEGIN

For the stamping, Bird Notes clear art stamps by Crafty Secrets were used, although you can substitute these for stamps of your own choosing.

Take the time to practise your stamping technique first on some scrap fabric until you are completely happy.

You can adapt the pocket sizes to fit your brushes; be sure to plan this out before you start.

JOOLES
OF SEW SWEET VIOLET

Jooles, a lover of sewing, other craftiness and eating cake, lives in West Sussex with her husband and her two gorgeous teenagers. A homebody, she loves nothing more than a whole day spent pootling away in her sewing room. Visit her blog at sewsweetviolet. blogspot.co.uk or discover more of her work at sewsweetviolet.etsy.com.

METHOD

{01} Make the ruffle

Cut a strip of fusible interfacing 50 x 3cm (20 x 1⅛in) and iron it onto the wrong side of the bird-printed fabric strip. Using the longest machine straight stitch and matching thread, sew down the centre. Pull one thread end to gather the fabric to just over 25cm (10in). Fasten the ends, even out the ruffles and press gently. Set aside.

{02} Prepare the pocket fabric

Take the 23 x 34cm (9 x 13½in) piece of linen (for the pocket) and fold it in half lengthwise; press. Pin then stitch the lace, then a 35cm (14in) length of the velvet ribbon, along the folded edge.

{03} Prepare the lining fabric

Cut a piece of fusible interfacing 25 x 32cm (10 x 12½in) and iron onto the wrong side of the same-sized piece of bird-printed fabric.

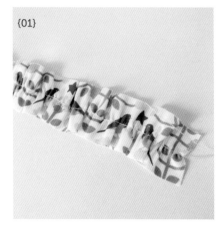

{01}

{04} Join the pocket fabric to the lining fabric

Place the pocket panel along the bottom edge of the lining fabric (right sides facing up), aligning the raw edges; allow a little overlap at each side. Insert a couple of pins to hold together, then turn over (wrong side up) and pin along the bottom and sides.

Sewing Story

I had fun experimenting with the making of the ruffle. I decided to back the fabric strip with fusible interfacing as this allows for just a pretty amount of fray, but as the fabric is stabilised by the interfacing, the fray won't go further. I also used fusible interfacing to back the bird-print lining fabric to make for stronger pockets for durability.
Jooles of Sew Sweet Violet

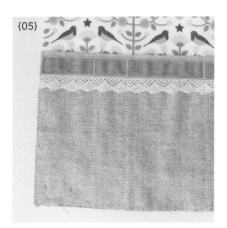

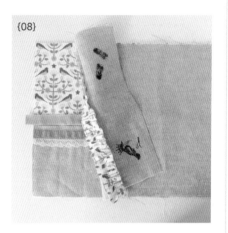

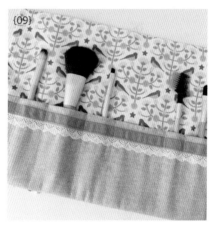

{05} Mark and stitch the pockets

Continuing to work on the wrong side, use a pencil and ruler to draw the stitching lines for the pockets (six lines will give seven pockets). Starting with the centre-most line, and using natural coloured thread, start stitching from the bottom edge until you can feel the top of the pocket; and then follow the stitching line back down again.

Now stitch down each side of the pocket strip just a little way from the edges, then trim the excess fabric.

{06} Attach the ruffle to the backing fabric

Take the second piece of linen (the backing) and use pins to mark a line 7cm (2¾in) up from one short end; pin on the ruffle and stitch along its centre.

{07} Stamp the bird design

Firmly stamp the inked up bird onto the fabric below the ruffle. Use a sticky note to mask off the bird's body, then stamp the crown onto its head. Stamp the feathers. Use an iron to heat set the stamped images on the wrong side of the fabric.

{08} Assemble and stitch the brush roll layers

Lay the cotton wadding on a flat surface, then place the pocket layer on top with the right side facing up. Fold the remaining velvet ribbon in half, right sides together and place the fold just above the pocket at the left-hand edge. Lay the front layer on top, right side down and stamped edge to the left. Pin all the way around and then stitch 1cm (⅜in) from the edge, leaving a gap for turning.

{09} Finish the brush roll

Trim the corners, then turn the right way out and press. Hand stitch the opening closed using slipstitch. Fill the pockets with brushes, roll the brush roll up and tie the ribbon in a bow to secure.

Hedgehog sewing set

This sweet sewing set includes a cute hedgehog pin cushion, a leaf-shaped needlecase so that your sewing needles are always close at hand, and little acorns to attach to your embroidery scissors. The tweed fabrics perfectly capture the woodland vibe and provide invaluable practise for sewing on wool weave fabrics.

MATERIALS

Tweed fabric: one piece 12.5 x 20cm (5 x 8in) for hedgehog body, one piece 18 x 25.5cm (7 x 10in) for leaf and offcuts for acorns

One piece of wool fabric 15cm (6in) square for hedgehog head and belly

One piece of wadding 18 x 12.5cm (7 x 5in) for leaf

Embroidery threads: black, green and brown

Two small black beads for eyes

Polyester stuffing

Pins, sewing needle and long doll sewing needle

Scissors

Sewing machine

SIZE

Hedgehog pin cushion: approx 14.5cm (5⅝in) wide by 7.5cm (3in) high

Acorn leaf needlecase: approx 12cm (4¾in) wide by 14.5cm (5⅝in) long

Acorn scissor keeper: approx 4cm (1½in) wide by 4.5cm (1¾in) high

FEATURED TECHNIQUES

- Machine-stitching techniques [p. 110]
- Curved seams [p. 121]
- Stitching by hand: running stitch [p. 98]; satin stitch [p. 104]; slipstitch [p. 99]; whipstitch [p. 98]

THERESIA COOKSON

Theresia is a self-taught craftivist with many years' experience and she has contributed to many magazines and books worldwide. She recently moved from the UK to Melbourne, Australia, and you can find more of her work at www.strawberriesandcream.etsy.com.

METHOD: PIN CUSHION

{01} Cut the fabric pieces
Use the templates provided (p. 157) to cut two bodies from the tweed fabric, and one belly and two heads from the wool fabric.

{02} Assemble the head and body pieces
To make one side of the hedgehog, place together one head and one body piece and sew using a 6mm (¼in) seam allowance. Repeat for the remaining head and body pieces to make the other side.

{03} Join the sides, then attach them to the belly
Pin the sides together right sides facing and stitch from nose to tail, leaving the bottom open for the belly piece. Pin the belly piece to the body/

head, aligning the pointed end of the belly piece with the nose. Stitch together using a 6mm (¼in) seam allowance and leave a small opening along one side for stuffing.

{04} Stuff and finish
Remove the pins, clip into the seams taking care not to cut the stitches, and turn right side out. Stuff the hedgehog with polyester stuffing.

To attach the bead eyes, thread the long doll sewing needle with black embroidery thread and take it through the stuffing opening to bring it out at the desired position on the face; thread on the bead for the first eye position, and exit on the other side of the face to thread on the second bead eye.

Embroider the nose using black embroidery thread and small satin stitches; then stitch up the stuffing opening neatly with whipstitch.

Sewing Story

The inspiration for this project came from the hedgehogs that slept under the leaves during the day in our garden back in England and came out to play at night! Although Australia is now my home, I do miss these beautiful British creatures and this sewing set will always remind me of them. *Theresia Cookson*

{03}

{04}

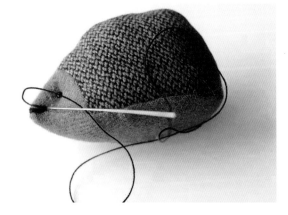

METHOD: NEEDLECASE

{01} Cut the fabric pieces
Use the templates provided (p. 157) to cut two leaves from the tweed fabric and one leaf slightly smaller from the wadding.

{02} Assemble the leaf pieces
Put the tweed fabric leaves right sides together, then place the wadding on top. Stitch the leaf layers together around the edges leaving a small opening. Clip the curved edges carefully, turn the leaf inside out and hand stitch the opening closed.

{03} Embroider and finish the leaf
Use green and brown embroidery thread to backstitch the leaf details if you choose to. Fold the leaf in half and stitch 2.5cm (1in) in from the end to make the leaf curve.

METHOD: SCISSORS KEEPER

{01} Cut the fabric pieces
Use the templates provided (p. 157) to cut two bottoms and one top for each acorn.

{02} Sew and stuff the bottom pieces
Place the acorn bottom pieces together with right sides facing; stitch around the edge leaving the top open and then turn right side out. Sew long running (gathering) stitches around the top opening, stuff firmly, pull up (not too tightly) and sew closed.

{03} Sew and stuff the top pieces
Sew a line of gathering stitches around the edge of the acorn top and pull up to leave an opening; stuff loosely, pull together and stitch closed.

{04} Join the acorn top to the acorn bottom
Place the acorn top on the acorn bottom and attach with slipstitch using green embroidery thread (this is quite tricky and requires concentration). Once the embroidery is complete leave a long length of thread for tying the acorn to the handle of the scissors.

Following steps 1–4, make another acorn, then tie the long thread ends to one of the handles to finish.

{02 + 03}

{04}

Trapeze sundress

{ *When you want to wear something that is feminine and playful, yet comfortable and easy-going, the A-line trapeze sundress is the perfect choice. It is super-cute worn during the day over a T-shirt or light sweater and goes so well with sneakers. Best of all, it's an absolute breeze to make.*

MATERIALS

2m (2⅛yd) of 140cm (55in) wide fabric

Pattern cutting paper, pens and pencil

Tape measure, long ruler and (optional) French curve

Pins and scissors

Iron

Sewing machine

SIZE

Custom fit to your measurements

FEATURED TECHNIQUES

- French seam [p. 123]
- Making a bias binding [p. 136]
- Machine-stitched hem [p. 125]

BEFORE YOU BEGIN

The trapeze sundress is designed to be drafted to each individual's measurements, resulting in a perfectly bespoke fit every time, so your first job is to draft your custom-fit pattern. You'll find this job easier if you invest in some pattern cutting paper (see note, p. 92).

When taking the measurements you need to draft your simple pattern, it is a good idea to enlist the help of a friend to ensure accuracy.

When selecting a fabric for your dress, choose something with body and drape – viscose crepe, or any light- to medium-weight viscose is ideal. Elisalex made her dress from Blossom viscose by fabric designer Atelier Brunette.

If you plan on making a longer dress than the garment shown, you may require more fabric.

Pre-wash your fabric to ensure it won't shrink the first time you wash the finished garment. Press as necessary.

Rather than making your own bias binding as for the garment shown, you could use a shop bought bias binding to contrast with your main fabric.

METHOD

Note: For pattern drafting steps 1 and 2, measurements have been given in inches to match markings on the pattern cutting paper.

{01} Drafting the front pattern

Cut a big piece of pattern cutting paper and start by drawing a straight vertical line approximately 30in long. This is the centre front.

From the top of the centre front line, draw a horizontal line that measures the distance between your bra straps divided by 2 and minus 1in. This is your front neckline.

Next, measure the distance between just below your collarbone down to the fullest part of your bust, and working from the top of the centre front line, mark this measurement onto your vertical line. From this point, draw a second horizontal line out that measures your full bust measurement plus 4in, divided by 4. This is your bust line.

Now measure the distance between your full bust and hip, again marking this point onto the centre front (vertical) line from the bust line. From here, draw a third horizontal line out that measures your hip measurement multiplied by 1.3, divided by 4. This is your hip line.

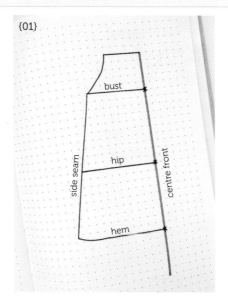

{01}

Decide on the final length you want your dress to be – neckline to hem – and mark this point down the centre front (vertical) line. Now, still working on the vertical line, measure the distance between the bust point and the hem. Draw a straight, diagonal line connecting the horizontal bust line to the hip line, continuing down for the same distance as the bust-hem measurement you just took. This is the side seam.

Draw a final horizontal line (this may need to curve ever so gently as you approach the side seam) connecting the side seam and centre front (vertical) line. This is your hemline.

Using a French curve (see note on p. 92), or your best hand-drawn

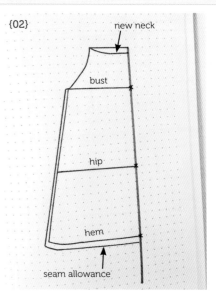

{02}

curve (but not too concave – keep it subtle!), connect the neckline to the side seam. This is your armhole.

{02} Finishing the front pattern

From the centre front, and coming down about an inch from the top, redraw your neckline so that it curves up gently to meet the top of the armhole.

Finally, add on seam allowances of 1.5cm (⅝in) down the side seams and 2.5cm (1in) along the hem. Note: no seam allowances are added to the neckline or armhole as these will be finished using bias binding.

{03} Cutting out the front pattern

Your dress front pattern piece is now complete. For future

{04}

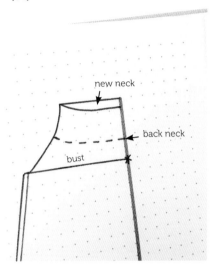

new neck

back neck

bust

reference, label it with the following information: the pattern's name, the measurements it has been drafted to, how much seam allowance has been included, and an indication that the centre front is to be cut 'on the fold'. Now cut it out.

{04} Drafting the back pattern

Now you need to trace your pattern piece off onto a second piece of pattern cutting paper to create the back pattern piece, adapting the height of the neckline as follows: for the back neckline, simply draw a new soft curve similar to that of the front neckline, about two thirds of the way down between the neckline and bust line (see dotted line). On the back pattern piece, the vertical line is your centre back line.

{05} Cut out your dress front and back

Fold your fabric in half lengthways, right sides together, and place your pattern pieces with the centre front and centre back lines on the fold of the fabric. Pin in place and carefully cut out each piece. Cut the fabric with your scissors to the left of the paper pattern pieces: this helps you to get a more accurate cut and lifts/distorts the fabric much less as you go.

{06} Cut out your bias binding strips

Working at a 45-degree angle from the selvage, cut two strips that measure 4cm (1½in) and approximately 140cm (55in) long for your shoulder strap ties. You will also need another two shorter 4cm (1½in) wide strips, one long enough to bind the front neckline and another long enough to bind the back neckline.

ELISALEX
OF BY HAND LONDON

Co-founder and Head of Design at indie sewing pattern company By Hand London, Elisalex de Castro Peake has been sewing since her late teens. Together with Charlotte Hintzen, Elisalex runs the creative side of BHL, designing and sampling new patterns, creating blog content and teaching classes. You can find their full collection of sewing patterns, plus a whole host of tutorials and inspiration at www.byhandlondon.com, and on Instagram @byhandlondon or @elisalex.

Sewing Story

Looking back on the years since Charlotte and I began BHL in 2008, I can't believe my luck – I get to spend my days making (and keeping) my dream wardrobe, designing patterns and seeing them come to life at the hands of our wondrous customers the world over, teaching and hopefully inspiring others to discover the joy of sewing. Then there's the host of talented people I've met along the way. In fact, I'd go so far as to say that it's the sunny, supportive nature of the global sewing community that is my driving force every day. *Elisalex de Castro Peake*

{07} Sew the side seams

French seams (see p. 123) are used to sew up the side seams, which results in a flawless finish without any unsightly raw edge seam allowances.

Place the dress front on top of the dress back, wrong sides together, and pin the side seams to secure. Stitch the side seams with a scant 6mm (¼in) seam allowance and press the seams open (or off to one side). Turn the dress inside out so that right sides are facing and press again. Pin the side seams to secure and stitch the side seams once more, this time with a 1cm (⅜in) seam allowance, to bring your total seam allowance to the full 1.5cm (⅝in). Press the seams towards the centre back.

{08} Bind the edges of the front and back neckline

Taking one of the shorter strips of the bias binding, pin the binding to the front neckline with the right side of the binding facing the wrong side of the neckline, see (08a) opposite. Stitch with a 6mm (¼in) seam allowance. Turn the dress through to the right side and press the seam in to the binding.

Now press the unstitched raw edge of the binding in by 6mm (¼in). Fold the binding over to the front of the dress and press (thereby creating a new fold down

{08a}

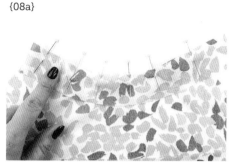

{08b}

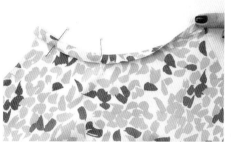

{09a}

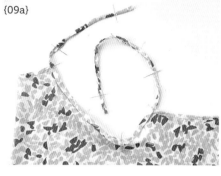

{08c}

{09b}

the centre of the binding). Make sure that the first line of stitching is covered, and pin the binding in place (08b).

Stitch neatly as close to the fold of the binding as you can, and trim away any excess binding at either end of the neckline (08c).

Repeat for the back neckline.

{09} Bind the armholes and make the shoulder strap ties

Binding the armholes is much the same as binding the front and back neckline, but this time, instead of trimming away the excess binding, you continue to fold, press and stitch it in order to create the shoulder strap ties.

Working one armhole at a time, start by aligning the centre of the shoulder strap binding with the underarm/side seam and pin that point first (right side of binding to wrong side of dress).

Continue to pin the binding to the armhole either side of the side seam and then stitch using a 6mm

(¼in) seam allowance. Press the seam up into the binding and then continue pressing in the bottom raw edge of the binding along the straps. Press in the top unstitched edges of the binding by 6mm (¼in) also.

Now fold and press the entire length of binding in half lengthways, pinning the straps to secure and pinning the binding into place at the armhole (09a).

Starting at one end of your shoulder strap, carefully stitch along the open folded edge to seal the binding, continuing along the

armhole and carrying on along the other shoulder strap length.

Tie a little knot at the end of each of the shoulder strap ties to finish (09b).

{10} Fit the dress

Now it's time to try the dress on, to mark the pleat that will shape the back of the dress – enlist the help of a friend if possible. First, tie or pin your shoulder straps at the point where you want the neckline (both front and back) to sit. The front neckline is designed to be high, skimming your collar-bone ideally, so aim for that and adjust accordingly to your body: the main thing is to get the neckline at the perfect height so that the armholes sit right – too low and they will gape.

Next, create the little box pleat at the centre back: pinch out however much you want to cinch the back neckline in by and pin; take off the dress and adjust to create a perfectly even and centred pleat, bringing the binding either side of the centre back in to meet at the centre to give you a sort of upside down V.

Pin the pleat in place and secure it by stitching along the line of your binding stitches.

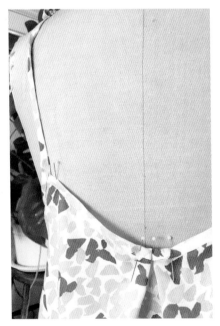

{11} Hem the dress
Press the hemline in by 1.3cm (½in) and then again by the same amount, or adjust to achieve your desired length. Stitch the hem into place and give your dress one final press to finish.

Take three tees

Three quick T-shirt makeovers to build your confidence when sewing stretchy knitted fabric. The colour block peplum tee transforms three shapeless T-shirts into a fun, feminine top; the fringed crop tee is festival-ready in less than half an hour; and your favourite floral prints jazz up a plain T-shirt for the heart pocket tee.

MATERIALS

Colour block peplum tee
Three T-shirts: two in one colour and one in another

Fringed crop tee
One T-shirt (or use leftover cut-off T-shirt from the peplum tee)

Approx 1m (1yd) of tasselled fringing

Heart pocket tee
One T-shirt

Cotton floral-print fabric, 40cm (16in) square to make bias binding

Pins, pinking shears, scissors and tape measure

Sewing machine and stretch needle

Iron

FEATURED TECHNIQUES

- Sewing on different fabrics: stretch fabric [p. 116]
- Straight stitch gathering [p. 135]
- Joining gathered and flat fabric [p. 136]
- Attaching fringe trims [p. 134]
- Making a bias binding [p. 136]
- Joining binding strips [p. 137]
- Binding a curved edge [p. 138]
- Topstitching [p. 113]

DESIGNED BY
THE NEW CRAFT HOUSE

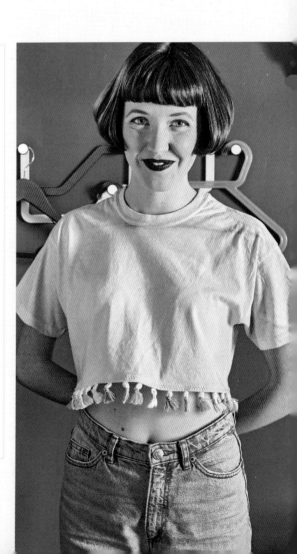

BEFORE YOU BEGIN

If you can't find T-shirts in your desired colours, dye plain white tees to your chosen shades. Hannah and Rosie used Dylon fabric dyes in Powder Pink and Sunflower Yellow for the colour block peplum tee.

Be careful when picking your fabrics for the heart pocket tee: don't choose anything too bulky or stiff to avoid adding too much bulk to the neck and armholes. Hannah and Rosie used a fine cotton lawn for their bias binding.

When sewing T-shirt fabric you are going to need to work with a stretch needle in your sewing machine, which is suitable for sewing knit fabric.

Sewing Story

We've always been big fans of customising clothes and a T-shirt is the perfect start point. We began our sewing journey with projects just like these, and they helped us to gain confidence with sewing machine techniques before we progressed onto patterns. We love that these three quick ideas can give new life to tired T-shirts as we're both huge believers in recycling and reusing!

Hannah and Rosie

METHOD: COLOUR BLOCK PEPLUM TEE

{01} Cut up your T-shirts

Take three T-shirts, one in the colour you'd like to use for the top body of your T-shirt transformation and two in your chosen colour for the peplum trim at the base of the T-shirt. Use pinking shears to cut off the bottom 20cm (8in) from each of the T-shirts (you can cut off more or less depending on how long you want your finished tee to be). Set aside the bottom of the top body T-shirt and the tops of the peplum trim T-shirts.

{02} Prepare the peplum strip

Taking your two T-shirt pieces for the peplum trim, cut open each piece at one of the side seams and cut out the old seam. With right sides facing, pin the two pieces together at each short end and stitch together using a 1.5cm (⅝in) seam allowance working with a stretch stitch.

Now work gathering stitches along one long edge of your joined peplum strip: starting and ending about 5cm (2in) from each end, sew a line of long straight stitches 1cm (⅜in) in from the raw edge, and be sure to leave long ends on your threads.

{03} Gather the peplum strip

Pull gently on the long threads to gather your fabric. Continue to gather until the peplum piece measures the same length as the circumference of the bottom of your top body piece (see photo below).

{04} Sew the peplum to the top body

With right sides together pin your peplum hoop around the bottom of your T-shirt body, matching up the raw edges; be sure to use lots of pins to ensure the gathers don't move around. Stitch together with a 1.5cm (⅝in) seam allowance using a stretch stitch. Press the seam allowance towards the body.

{03}

METHOD: FRINGED CROP TEE

{01} Prepare the hem

Using one of the set aside tops from step 1 of the peplum tee, fold over the hem by 1cm (³⁄₈in) and then again by 1cm (³⁄₈in); press and pin in place. (Alternatively, cut off the bottom 20cm (8in) of your chosen T-shirt and hem as described.)

{02} Add the tassel trim and stitch

Position your tassel trim over the pressed hem on the wrong side of the T-shirt, and line it up so that the tassels poke over the edge of the hem but make sure that the trim tape cannot be seen. Pin in place, overlapping the ends of the tape by 2cm (5in). Using a zigzag stitch (or another stretch stitch), sew the trim and hem in place. (If you wish, you can add tassel trim to the sleeves, too, although you will need to buy a little more trim for this.)

METHOD: HEART POCKET TEE

{01} Make the bias binding
Fold your square of floral-print fabric in half diagonally and cut along the fold, which is on the bias of the fabric. Cut 5cm (2in) wide strips on the bias and sew into one length, long enough to go around the neck and sleeves of your T-shirt.

Fold your joined fabric strip in half wrong sides together and press. Open up, and then press each edge into the centre fold. Refold along the centre fold and press again.

{02} Attach the bias binding to the neck and sleeves
Using pinking shears, trim off the neckband and armhole seams from your T-shirt.

Pin the bias binding around the neckline of your T-shirt, folding it over the edge of the neckline so that no raw edges can be seen. Stitch the bias binding in place, working as close to the edge of the binding as you can. Attach the bias binding to the sleeves in the same way.

{03} Cut and prepare the heart pocket
Cut out a heart shape from floral-print fabric using the template provided on p. 149. Carefully press the edges of the heart in by 5mm (3/16in), clipping into the curves with small-bladed scissors to allow the fabric to turn smoothly.

Topstitch around the top curves of your heart 2mm (3/32in) from the edge, between the marks shown on the photo below.

{04} Sew the heart pocket in place
Position your heart where you'd like it be on your T-shirt and pin it in place. Stitch around the bottom half of the heart 2mm (3/32in) from the edge, backstitching at the start and end of your stitching.

{01}

{02}

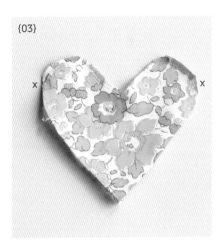

{03}

Badger pillow

Bring a touch of sweet woodland charm to your home with this adorable badger pillow. Made of felt, this character design is simple enough to finish in an afternoon, and it can even be stitched by hand using a small, neat backstitch if you don't have a sewing machine.

MATERIALS

Two pieces of black felt 30.5 x 23cm (12 x 9in)

One piece of white felt 10 x 15cm (4 x 6in)

Two black 12mm (½in) safety eyes with washers

One black 15mm (⅝in) safety nose with washer

Polyester toy stuffing

Sewing threads: white and black

Scissors

Sewing needle and pins

Sewing machine

SIZE

25.5cm (10in) wide x 20.5cm (8in) high

FEATURED TECHNIQUES

- Machine-stitching techniques [p. 110]
- Curved seams [p. 121]
- Stitching by hand: slipstitch [p. 99]

BEFORE YOU BEGIN

Felt is one of the easiest materials to work with as the edges of the fabric do not fray when cut, and this simple design can be completely stitched by hand if you choose to.

Decide if you want your badger to face left or right; Laura chose to have hers facing right, but you could just as easily have yours facing left. Or make one facing right and one facing left for a matching pair to bookend your sofa.

The finished pillow measures 25.5 x 20.5cm (10 x 8in), but the templates can easily be enlarged again to make a really big badger pillow.

METHOD

{01} Cut the felt pieces

Using the templates provided (p. 151), cut the following shapes from your felt fabrics: two black bodies, one white face, and one right and one left white ear.

{02} Assemble the front of the badger

Pin the white face shape to one of the black body shapes so that the top of the face lines up with the top of the head, centring it between the ears. Pin the white ear shapes onto the black body as seen in the photo below, centring them about 2.5cm (1in) from the edge. Using white thread, machine stitch the face and ears to the body.

Use sharp, pointed scissors to pierce small holes for the safety eyes and nose, making the holes only as wide as the shank for the plastic pieces. Insert the eyes and nose and fasten with the washers.

{03} Join the front and back pieces

Match up the front and back body pieces with right sides facing, and pin together. Using black thread, sew around the edge with a 1cm (³⁄₈in) seam allowance, leaving a small opening approximately 7.5cm (3in) along one of the straight parts of the body. Trim excess fabric around the seam and clip small notches into the curved areas, taking care not to cut into the seam. This will help reduce bulk and make for a smoother shape at the curves.

{04} Stuff and finish

Turn the badger right side out and gently push out the shapes of the ears and feet with the eraser end of a pencil. Begin adding the stuffing, starting with the area farthest from the opening. To avoid lumps in the finished piece, it is best to fill slowly, using small handfuls of stuffing.

Flip the badger over periodically as you stuff to check both sides for any signs of unevenness.

Once your badger is stuffed to your liking, slipstitch the opening closed with black thread doubled on the needle for a secure seam (you can add a little more stuffing as you stitch so that the badger is uniformly filled).

LAURA FISHER

Laura is a recent college grad, living in California, who loves creating things that make people smile. She enjoys being a handmade artist because of how fulfilling it is to see an idea come to life. Find her online at www.fluffedanimals.etsy.com.

Trimmed Christmas stocking

To make the mix and match stocking you can use festive fabrics, or team your favourite floral-print fabrics with bargain vintage finds. Finish off with your choice of embellishments, from ricrac to yo-yo flowers. Hang above the fireplace, and – fingers-crossed – your stocking will soon be full of gorgeous gifts.

MATERIALS

Main fabric: approx 0.25m (¼yd) for each stocking

Lining fabric: approx 0.25m (¼yd) for each stocking

Contrasting fabrics: use up your fabric leftovers

Trimmings: ribbons, ricrac, lace, buttons, doilies

Scissors

Sewing machine

Sewing needle

Pins

SIZE

Approx 44cm (17in) long

FEATURED TECHNIQUES

- Machine-stitching techniques [p.110]
- Attaching in-seam trims [p. 135]
- Curved seams [p. 121]
- Self-covering buttons [p. 133]

DESIGNED BY
JANE HUGHES

BEFORE YOU BEGIN

Total fabric requirement for the main body of each stocking including lining is approximately 0.5m (½yd). You could use the same fabric for both main body and lining if you choose to, although it's more fun to mix and match, especially if you are making a stocking for each member of your family.

METHOD

{01} Cut out your fabrics

Gather together your materials, choosing fabric and trimmings that complement each other. Trace the templates on p. 151 on to a piece of paper and cut out to make your stocking patterns.

Fold your main fabric neatly in half, and using template A cut out two stocking shapes.

Fold your lining fabric and cut out two more stocking shapes.

Using templates B, C and D, cut out one of each shape in your contrasting fabrics for your stocking top, toe and heel.

{02} Sew the stocking top in place

Press a 1cm (³⁄₈in) hem at the bottom edge of the stocking top. Lay one main stocking piece flat, with right side facing you, and pin the stocking top in place; add an in-seam lace trim if you choose to. Machine stitch the stocking top onto the main stocking piece. Now stitch any ribbon, lace or ricrac trims to the stocking top, pinning them in place before sewing on.

{03} Sew the heel and toe in place

Next take your heel and toe pieces, pin in place, then sew onto the stocking. Use a zigzag stitch for added embellishment.

{04} Sew the stocking back and front together

Take both main stocking pieces and pin right sides together. Machine stitch using a 1cm (³⁄₈in) seam allowance, trim edges and snip into curves to allow for neat turning. Turn the stocking right way out and press a 1.5cm (⁵⁄₈in) hem around the top.

{05} Add the lining

Taking the two lining pieces, pin and machine stitch right sides together with a 1cm (³⁄₈in) seam allowance. Trim and snip seams (as step 4) but do not turn right way out. Press a 1.5cm (⁵⁄₈in) hem along the top. Place the lining inside the main stocking.

{06} Add a hanging loop and finish

Take a piece of ribbon approx 16cm (6¼in) long, fold in half and place the ends in between the main stocking and stocking lining; pin in place. Work a line of machine stitch around the top of the stocking 6mm (¼in) from the edge, and press to finish.

{07} Make a yo-yo flower {optional}

Cut a circle of fabric the size of a saucer and hand sew a running stitch along the edge all the way round. Draw up to gather the outside edge inwards and sew down in the centre.

Add a self-covered button (see p. 133) to the centre of the yo-yo flower and trim with ribbon. Sew the finished yo-yo flower onto the stocking top.

Opposite: If using a vintage doily for the toe and heel as on the right-hand stocking, cut the doily in half and shape the toe and heel using templates C and D as a guide.

Dapper bear pyjama case

As well as keeping your pyjamas neat and tidy during the day, this smartly-dressed bear will also take care of your current bedtime read. With a super-soft felt face, his mouth is made from a simple set-in zip and his outfit can be co-ordinated to match your bedding or decor.

MATERIALS

Wool felt: one piece of pale grey 70cm (27½in) square, one piece of white 20cm (8in) square and one small piece of black

One piece of pale grey medium-weight cotton fabric 25 x 30cm (10 x 12in)

One piece of blue check medium-weight cotton fabric 35 x 90cm (13¾ x 35¼in)

One piece of red stripe medium-weight cotton fabric 35 x 60cm (13¾ x 23½in)

25cm (10in) white zip

Sewing threads: grey, black and white

Stranded cotton (floss): black and white

Fabric glue

Scissors

Lightweight fusible interfacing

Tape measure or ruler

Iron

Pins and embroidery needle

Sewing machine and zipper foot

Erasable fabric marker

Wadding or cotton wool

SIZE

Approx 30cm (12in) wide by 65cm (25½in) high

FEATURED TECHNIQUES

- Inserting a basic zip [p. 131]
- Stitching by hand: backstitch [p. 98]; French knots [p. 104]; running stitch [p. 98]; slipstitch [p. 99]
- Machine-stitching techniques [p. 110]
- Curved seams [p. 121]

BEFORE YOU BEGIN

Ideally, the fabrics you use for the bear's clothing should both be of a similar weight or thickness. However, if they're not, and you can't find a suitable alternative, don't despair! The red stripe fabric used here was quite a bit thinner than the blue check, so lightweight fusible interfacing was ironed onto the back of it to redress the balance and solve the problem.

Use a 1cm (⅜in) seam allowance throughout unless otherwise stated.

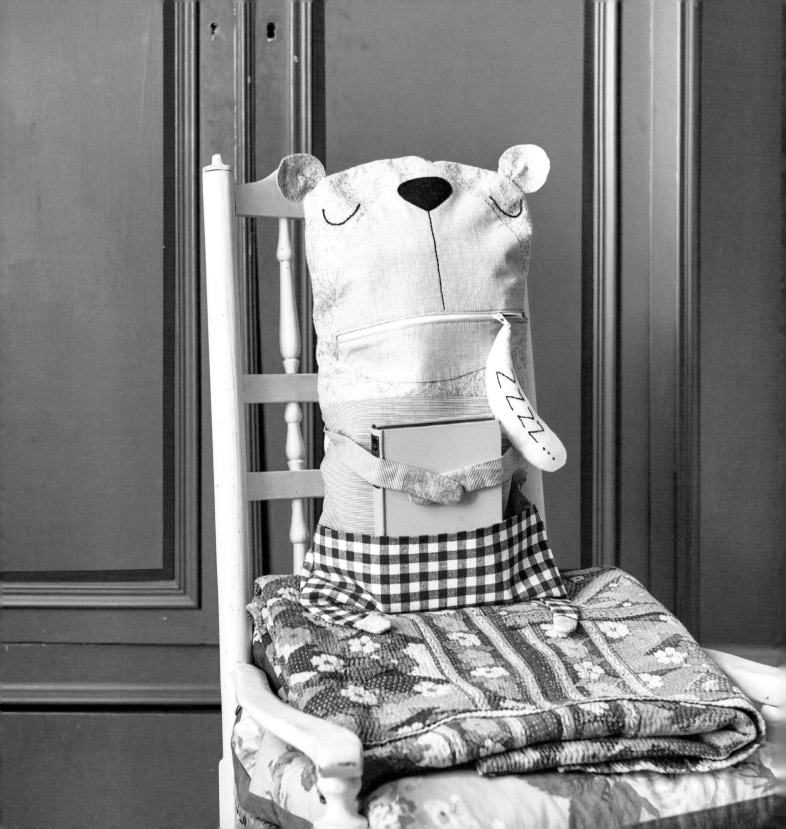

KIRSTY NEALE

Kirsty is an author, illustrator and maker, living in London. She enjoys working with fabric and thread, often combining new and vintage materials, and is very detail-focused (which is just a nice way of saying obsessive). Her work has been published in a variety of magazines and she has written several craft books. Visit www.kirstyneale.co.uk.

Sewing Story

My secret sewing confession is that I am a terrible felt snob! Most synthetic felts are stiff, scratchy and not much fun to work with – even the addition of a small amount of wool makes an enormous difference to the handle, and to your finished project. The grey wool used to make the dapper bear has a lovely heathered look, and with a wool content of around 30 per cent, it's both soft and affordable. Try searching online for 'wool felt', rather than just 'felt' if you want to find something similar.
Kirsty Neale

{02}

METHOD

{01} Cut out the fabric pieces
Use the templates provided on p. 156 to cut out the following pieces:
From grey wool felt: two head pieces, two ears, two hands and two feet.

From grey cotton: one upper snout, one lower snout, two hands and two feet.
From blue check cotton: two leg sections and one leg (pocket) section.
From black wool felt: one nose.
From white wool felt: two speech bubbles.

{02} Prepare the front head piece for zip insertion
Cut a 28 x 6cm (11 x 2⅜in) strip of fusible interfacing and iron it onto the reverse of one of the grey wool head pieces, in the position marked on the template. Cut a narrow slit in the interfaced felt as marked on the template.

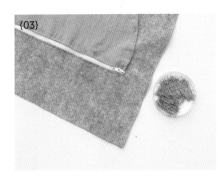
{03}

{05}

{03} Insert zip and add snout

Place the zip underneath the slit, lining up the zip slider at the right-hand end. Hand stitch with backstitch along both sides of the zip to hold it in place – the stitches don't need to be especially neat, as they will be hidden when the snout is sewn in place.

Fold over and pin a 5mm ($^3/_{16}$in) hem around the curved edges of the upper snout and continue along the straight edge. Pin the snout to the top edge of the zip only, taking care to pin through both felt and zip tape. Using a zipper foot, sew along the straight edge, then slipstitch the remaining edges of the snout by hand; press. Repeat to attach the lower snout in the same way. Turn to the wrong side and add a little fabric glue to each end of the zip tape to adhere it to the underside of the felt.

{04} Complete the facial details

Stitch the nose towards the top of the upper snout, using black thread and small running stitches. Sew a line of backstitches from the nose down to the zip mouth, using four strands of black embroidery thread. With an erasable fabric marker, draw two 'U' shapes either side of the snout for the bear's eyes and backstitch as before.

{05} Make the ears

Referring to the ear template, fold line A over line B to make a small pleat on each ear and tack to hold in place. Pin an ear to each side of the head, right sides facing (see head template for placement).

{06} Make the arms and the upper body

Start with the arms: cut two 3.5 x 20cm ($1^3/_8$ x 8in) red stripe fabric pieces for each arm. With right sides facing, sew a grey felt hand to the end of one piece and a grey cotton hand to the end of the other; press seams towards the red stripe fabric. Pin the two arm pieces together, right sides facing, then stitch with a 5mm ($^3/_{16}$in) seam allowance (standard presser foot) leaving the short end open for turning. Clip around the curved edges of the hand. Turn through, then press. Make a second arm in the same way. (The arms will be joined to the upper body in step 8.)

Cut two 17 x 32cm ($6^3/_4$ x $12^1/_2$in) rectangles of red stripe fabric for the upper body. Stitch one upper body to the front head and the other to the back head. Press the seams towards the stripe fabric.

{07} Make the lower body

Take the leg (pocket) section and iron a 10 x 32cm (4 x $12^1/_2$in) piece of fusible interfacing to the wrong side of the upper section as shown on the template. Fold along the dotted line, as marked, so the interfacing is hidden between the two layers of fabric.

With right sides facing, sew a felt foot to the end of each leg, then press the seams towards the check fabric. Take one of the check fabric leg sections and stitch a cotton foot to the end of each leg.

{08} Complete the bear back and front and join together

With right sides facing, stitch the top edge of the leg section (with feet) to the bottom edge of the red stripe fabric to form the back of the bear.

Take the remaining leg section (without feet) and sew this to the bottom of the red stripe fabric to form the front of the bear.

Pin and then tack the leg (pocket) piece directly over the top of the front legs, so the wrong side of the leg (pocket) piece is against the right side of the leg piece. Line up the folded edge of the pocket with the seam between the legs and body.

Place the arms over the front of the body, angling them so the hands cross over in the centre. Pin the top of the arms to the sides of the body.

Open the zip, then pin the front and back of the bear, right sides together, around the edges. Sew through all layers of fabric, catching in the ears and arms as you go. Clip curves to ease the fabric, then turn the right way out through the unzipped mouth, and press all the way around the edges.

Remove any tacking stitches and slipstitch the bear's hands together to keep them wrapped around any book placed in the pocket.

{09} Make the plush zip pull

Copy the 'zzzz...' text onto one of the speech bubble pieces with an erasable fabric marker. Stitch the letters with backstitch and work the dots with French knots, using three strands of black embroidery thread.

Sew the two speech bubble pieces together, with right sides facing, leaving a small gap at the bottom edge for turning. Turn through and press; gently stuff with wadding or cotton wool, then slipstitch the opening shut. Securely sew the pointed end of the speech bubble to the hole in the zip pull tab using white embroidery thread. Knot the thread and trim.

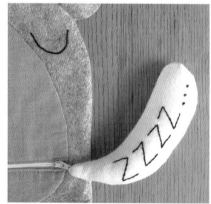

Foxy sleep mask

Get your beauty sleep and look effortlessly foxy at the same time with this fun mask made from felt and orange-print fabric. It can be stitched either by hand or machine, and be sure to choose a super-soft wool felt so that it is comfortable to wear for an afternoon nap.

MATERIALS

Two pieces of orange-print fabric
25.5 x 15cm (10 x 6in)

One piece of white felt 30.5cm (12in)
square

Small pieces of black and pale pink felt

Embroidery threads: white, black and
pale pink

1m (1⅛yd) narrow ribbon

Sewing thread and needle

Water-erasable fabric pen

Scissors and pins

Iron

Sewing machine (optional)

DESIGNED BY
KIRSTY NEALE

SIZE

Approx 18cm (7in) wide by
12cm (4¾in) high

FEATURED TECHNIQUES

- Stitching by hand: backstitch [p. 98];
  slipstitch [p. 99]; French knots
  [p. 104]; whipstitch [p. 98]
- Machine-stitching techniques [p. 110]
- Curved seams [p. 121]
- Trimming to neaten seams [p. 119]

BEFORE YOU BEGIN

You'll love the luxury of the silky ribbon ties of the foxy sleep mask, but if you are a night-time rock and roller, or if you'd prefer a snugger fit, you might want to substitute elastic to keep the sleep mask in place. If so, simply cut a strip of elastic to fit snugly around your head, and pin the ends to each side before stitching the layers together.

METHOD

{01} Make the upper head

Trace the upper head template (p. 152) onto the reverse of one of your pieces of orange-print fabric pieces. Cut it out very roughly, leaving 3cm (1⅛in) all the way around, then pin it to the second piece of orange-print fabric with right sides facing. Sew around the outline to join the two pieces together using either a machine straight stitch or a neat backstitch if stitching by hand, leaving a gap at the top edge for turning.

Trim the excess fabric to leave 1cm (⅜in) all the way around. Clip into the corners and along the curved edges to ease the seams. Turn the upper head the right way out through the gap, and press to neaten. Slipstitch the turning gap closed.

{02} Cut the felt pieces

Using the templates provided (p. 152), cut two heads and two inner ears from white felt, two cheeks from pink felt and a nose from black felt. Draw eyes onto one of the head pieces using the water-erasable fabric pen.

{03} Embroider the eyes

Use black embroidery thread and backstitch to stitch over the marked outline of each eye, then work

medium-length straight stitches out from the closed eye outline for the eyelashes.

{04} Assemble the mask

Place one pink cheek section on each side of the face, lining up the lower edges. Sew in place with small whipstitches, leaving the lower edges open for now. Sew a white inner ear onto each side of the printed fabric upper head section.

Cut two 40cm (14in) lengths of ribbon and pin one end of each piece to either side of the head. Place the two white felt head pieces together, so the ribbon ends are sandwiched in between, then add the printed fabric upper head

on top. Sew neatly along all edges to join the pieces securely together, using threads to match the fabrics.

Finally, stitch the black felt nose into place.

{05} Finish the embroidery

Add about seven French knots to either side of the black felt nose to represent the whiskers.

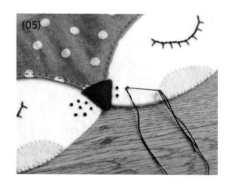

Sewing Story

Our neighbours have both a family of urban foxes and a particularly sensitive security light in their back garden. Taking inspiration from the former to combat the super bright, sleep-disrupting effects of the latter seemed like an obvious solution.

Kirsty Neale

Fruity floor cushions

This collection, inspired by our favourite citrus fruit slices, provides fun, informal seating when friends come around. These floor cushions are a great way to bring a splash of colour to your living room but they can be easily stacked when not in use. They'll also give you plenty of practise to get to grips with zips.

MATERIALS (FOR EACH CUSHION)

1.15m (1¼yd) of 115cm (45in) wide bright coloured cotton fabric

1.15m (1¼yd) of 115cm (45in) wide pastel coloured cotton fabric

50cm (20in) of double-sided fusible webbing

3m (3¼yd) of piping cord

55cm (22in) zip

Old duvet for stuffing

Ruler and tape measure

Sewing machine with piping foot (optional) and zipper foot

Scissors and seam ripper

Pins and quilting clips

Iron

SIZE

55cm (22in) wide by 20cm (8in) deep

FEATURED TECHNIQUES

- Machine-stitching techniques [p. 110]
- Inserting a basic zip [p. 131]
- Machine appliqué [p. 143]
- Free-motion machine embroidery (p. 141)
- Corded piping [p. 140]
- Making bias binding [p. 136]
- Joining bias binding strips (p. 137)

SAMMY AND H

Sammy Claridge runs online fabric shop Sew Crafty and works as a freelance project designer. She and Heather Thomas (H) met at art college and have never looked back. They are best friends and blogging buddies who love all manner of crafty activities and handmade adventures. They share them all on their blog at www.liveitloveitmakeit.com.

Sewing Story

My mum taught me everything I know about fabric and sewing. She was a costumier in London back in the 1960s and has so many fun stories, but the practical skills that she passed on to me at a young age and her passion for fabric has been the thing that has stuck with me the most. **Sammy Claridge**

BEFORE YOU BEGIN

To make the floor cushions as shown 100 per cent cotton fabric was used, but you could easily use a thicker fabric, such as cotton drill or canvas.

Using a piping foot on your sewing machine will make inserting the corded piping much easier; alternatively use a zipper foot.

To use ready-made bias binding rather than make your own, purchase 3m (3¼yd) of 2.5cm (1in) bias binding to match your bright fabric.

Make paper pattern pieces to the measurements given in step 1 – baking paper is a great option for this.

To make a circle pattern, take a square of paper as big as the circle needs to be. Fold it in half, then into quarters. Take the radius measurement and use a ruler to mark out this distance from the centre fold, making your marks as close together as possible to create a quarter circle. Cut along this pencil line through all the layers, then unfold the paper to reveal a circle.

To make a semicircle shape pattern, make a circle pattern, fold it in a half and measure and mark a line 1.5cm (⅝in) from the foldline. Cut along the marked line and discard the smaller half of the semicircle shape.

Use a 1.5cm (⅝in) seam allowance throughout unless otherwise stated.

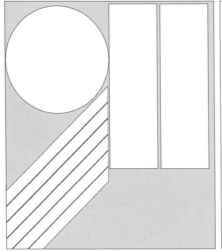
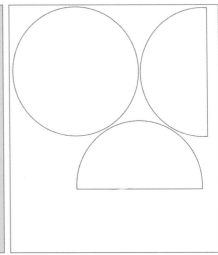

METHOD

{01} Mark out your fabrics
Referring to the layout diagrams above and using the paper patterns, mark out the following pieces:
From the bright fabric (above left): One 50cm (20in) diameter circle, two side panels measuring 75 x 23cm (29½ x 9in) and at least six 5cm (2in) wide strips at a 45-degree angle for the bias binding.
From the pastel fabric (above right): One 60cm (23½in) diameter circle and two semicircle shapes with a 60cm (23½in) width and a height of 31.5cm (12⅝in), which includes a 1.5cm (⅝in) seam allowance for the zip insertion.

{02} Prepare your fabric pieces
Carefully cut out all the marked up pieces from your fabrics.

Iron the fusible webbing onto the wrong side of the 50cm (20in) diameter circle.

{03} Make the corded piping
Join your bias binding strips to create one long strip (see p. 137). Cover the piping cord with your bias binding strip (see p. 140) and sew it in place using a piping foot if you have one (alternatively, use a zipper foot).

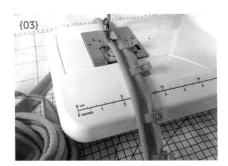

{03}

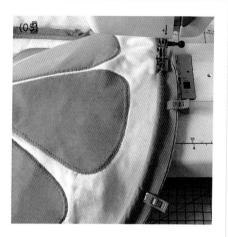

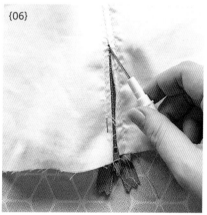

{04} Make and appliqué the fruit slice segments

Take your fusible-web backed fabric circle and cut it in half, then in half again, to give you quarters. Now cut each quarter in half to give you eight segments. Round off the corners of each segment and trim down all the way around by just a little (see photo above).

Remove the backing paper from the fusible webbing and carefully position each segment onto the larger, lighter (pastel) fabric circle to give the impression of a fruit slice. Iron the segments in place.

Once the fusible webbing has cooled, sew all the way around the segment pieces with zigzag stitch (standard presser foot) to finish the cushion top. Alternatively, use free-motion embroidery.

{05} Sew the corded piping to the cushion top

Take half of the corded piping length you have created and sew it in place around the edge of the cushion top (using a piping or zipper foot).

{06} Make the cushion base and insert zip

Take the two light fabric semicircle shapes and place together with right sides facing. Using a long (tacking) stitch, sew them together along the straight edge only. Press the seam open.

Still working on the wrong side of the fabric, take the zip and centre it over the join in the light fabric circle, right side down, and pin it in place. Turn the circle to the right side and sew all the way around the

zip (using a zipper foot), taking care to avoid the runner. Use a seam ripper to unpick the tacking stitches to reveal the zip. Unzip it halfway so that when you sew all the pieces together in step 7, you will be able to turn the cushion right side out through the opening.

Sew the remaining length of corded piping around the edge of the base (light fabric) circle, lining up the raw edges as before.

{07} Join the side panels and finish

Join the side panels together at the short ends to make a fabric hoop (using a standard presser foot). Sew the side panel to the top and bottom pieces matching up the raw edges using a piping or zipper foot.

Trim away any excess on the seams. Turn the cover right side out through the half-open zip, then open the zip fully and stuff the cover to complete the cushion: an old duvet makes an ideal filling, although you may need to cut it up.

{07}

Note

The basic shape and construction of this floor cushion can be used to make lots of different designs. If fruit isn't your thing, you can replace the segments with an icing appliqué and sequin sprinkles to make a donut cushion.

Great creative and hone your free-motion embroidery skills to appliqué the fruit slice segments to the top of your floor cushion as seen here on the lime version.

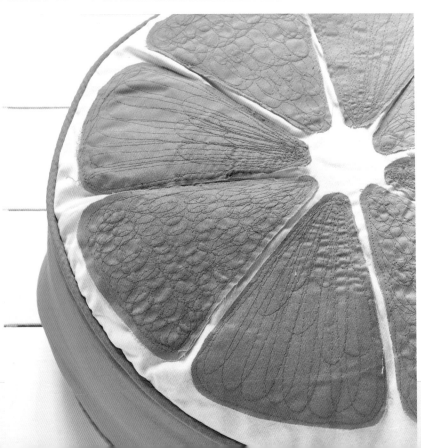

Hot water bottle covers

Snuggle up alongside your loved one with these matching hot water bottle covers made from sumptuous velvet for extra cosiness. Each is appliquéd with a fabric silhouette – for her a striding moose, for him an ambling bear. The size of the covers can be easily adapted to fit your hot water bottles.

MATERIALS (PER COVER)

Two pieces of velvet fabric 24.5 x 48.5cm (9¾ x 19¼in)

Printed fabric: two pieces 24.5 x 48.5cm (9¾ x 19¼in) for lining and one piece approx 15cm (6in) square for appliqué

Two pieces of wadding 24.5 x 48.5cm (9¾ x 19¼in)

One piece of felt approx 15cm (6in) square

Double-sided fusible webbing

1m (1⅛yd) velvet ribbon to co-ordinate with the printed fabric

50cm (20in) cotton lace trim (for her cover only)

Scissors

Iron and pressing cloth

Sewing machine

SIZE

For a hot water bottle cover measuring 18 x 30cm (7 x 12in)

FEATURED TECHNIQUES

- Machine-stitching techniques [p. 110]
- Fused appliqué [p. 143]
- Sewing on different fabrics: velvet [p. 116]
- Pressing: flat seams [p. 96]
- Stitching by hand: slipstitch [p. 99]

BEFORE YOU BEGIN

If your hot water bottle size differs from the size given, make a pattern for cutting your fabric pieces by laying the bottle on a piece of paper and adding 3.5cm (1⅜in) to each side and the bottom, and 15cm (6in) to the top.

DESIGNED BY
JOOLES
OF SEW SWEET VIOLET

METHOD

{01} Make the appliqué motif
Iron fusible webbing to the wrong side of the small printed fabric piece. Using the template provided (p. 158), cut out your motif from the fabric. Peel off the backing and iron the motif onto the felt, using the pressing cloth to protect the felt. Iron a piece of fusible webbing to the wrong side of the felt. Carefully cut around the fabric motif to leave a few millimetres of felt showing around the outline.

{02} Attach the appliqué motif to the velvet fabric
Peel off the backing from the motif and place it onto the right side of one of the velvet fabric pieces so the animal's feet are about 11cm (4¼in) from the bottom (short) edge; iron to attach. Machine stitch around the motif just inside the edge of the printed fabric: go slowly and lift the presser foot to turn the fabric leaving the needle in the down position each time you do so.

{03} Assemble the cover front
Place a piece of wadding on the wrong side of the decorated velvet fabric, then place these two fabric layers on top of one of the large printed fabric pieces with right sides together. Making

sure that the motif is facing the right way up (with the head end towards the top seam that you are about to sew), sew across the top edge with a 1cm (³⁄₈in) seam allowance. Unfold and press the seam using a pressing cloth.

{04} Assemble the cover back
To make the cover back, make a fabric sandwich as in step 3 with the remaining pieces of velvet fabric, wadding and printed fabric, ensuring that the velvet pile is going the same way on both the front and the back of the cover.

{05} Attach the lace trim
For her cover only, lay the lace on the lining fabric next to the seam and stitch in place.

{06} Join the front and back pieces
With the front and back cover pieces unfolded, place them together with right sides facing and take care to match seams. Pin very well and sew around the edges with a 1cm (³⁄₈in) seam allowance, leaving an opening in the lining (printed fabric) for turning.

Trim the seams, turn right side out and slipstitch the opening closed. Push the lining inside the cover, making sure to push it into the corners.

{07} Attach the ribbon tie
Pop your bottle inside the cover. Pin the centre point of the ribbon to the back cover at the bottle's neck. Remove the bottle and stitch the ribbon in place.

Replace the hot water bottle, fold down the top to make the cuff and tie the ribbon in a bow.

Sewing Story

My hot water bottle cover is basically a rectangle bag shape made from a luxurious mink velvet fabric lined with a liberty print. I made it high enough for a turn-down top to reveal the lining, and I've used a wide velvet ribbon tie to gather the neck of the cover around the hot water bottle. To decorate each cover, I used an animal silhouette cut from the lining fabric and attached to co-ordinating felt to give it a lovely raised look. **Jooles of Sew Sweet Violet**

Photo album cover

An album filled with photographs that capture memories of a special day makes the perfect gift for newlyweds. And a customised cover, decorated with a machine appliqué motif and a little hand embroidery in the wedding colours, brings back the emotions of the occasion at first glance, even before you take a peek inside!

MATERIALS

Photograph album 24cm (9½in) high by 21.5cm (8½in) wide by 1.8cm (¾in) deep

Cotton/linen blend fabric: two pieces 26 x 20.5cm (10¼ x 8¼in) for front and back cover and two pieces 26 x 12.5cm (10¼ x 5in) for inside panels

One piece of floral-print fabric 26 x 10cm (10¼ x 4in) for spine

One piece of floral-print fabric 26 x 47cm (10¼ x 18½in) for lining

Scraps of floral-print fabric for appliqué

Double-sided fusible webbing

Ribbon and embroidery threads in colours to match the floral-print fabrics

Good-quality black sewing thread

Embroidery hoop

Sewing machine and darning foot (optional)

Pencil

Iron

Scissors

Pins and embroidery needle

SIZE

For a cover to fit a photograph album measuring 24cm (9½in) high by 21.5cm (8½in) wide by 1.8cm (¾in) deep

FEATURED TECHNIQUES

- Machine-stitching techniques [p. 110]
- Fused appliqué [p. 143]
- Free-motion machine embroidery [p. 141]
- Transferring embroidery designs [p. 100]
- Stitching by hand: backstitch [p. 98]; detached chain stitch [p. 102]; French knots [p. 104]; running stitch [p. 98]; satin stitch [p. 104]; slipstitch [p. 99]

Note

To calculate the fabric needed to create a cover for a different sized photo album, measure the width of your album, double it, add the depth of the spine, then add a 1cm (³⁄₈in) seam allowance all around the edge.

EMILY CARLILL

Emily Carlill crafted her wedding in 2011, and she enjoyed it so much that she now makes items for other people's weddings, and she has expanded her sewing repertoire to include gifts for babies as well as keepsakes for the home. You can follow her blog a www.emilycarlill.com.

METHOD

{01} Attach the spine to the front fabric

Pin the floral-print fabric spine on top of the cotton/linen front piece with right sides facing, lining up along the left edge. Machine stitch using a 1cm (³⁄₈in) seam allowance. Press the seams open.

{02} Cut the appliqué pieces from floral-print fabric

Trace the birds, ribbon banner and heart templates (p. 153) onto pieces of double-sided fusible webbing. Use an iron to press the motifs onto the back of your chosen fabric scraps, then cut out carefully around the marked outlines.

{03} Position the appliqué pieces

Peel off the paper backing from the fusible webbing, position the motifs on the album cover front and iron in place.

{04} Machine appliqué the design

Hoop up the fabric and attach a darning foot (if you have one) to your sewing machine. Drop the machine's feed dog and, using the black thread, freehand machine embroider around the shapes twice. Add the shading on the ribbon banner, the eyes to the birds and the trailing ribbon to the hanging heart. Trim and neaten the threads at the front and back. Remove the hoop.

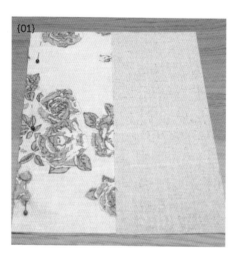

{01}

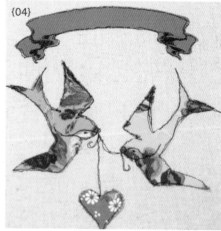

{04}

{05} Work the hand embroidery
Use a pencil to lightly mark the first names of the happy couple and the date of their wedding onto the ribbon banner. Use a light box (or hold the fabric up against a window) to trace the flower embroidery and corner motif patterns (see p. 153) onto the appliquéd fabric.

Use backstitch to embroider the names/date, and follow the stitch key on the embroidery patterns for working the flower embroidery and the corner motifs in thread colours to match your fabrics.

Complete the running stitch border all the way around the edge of the cover.

{06} Join the back piece
With right sides facing, pin the cotton/linen back piece to the raw edge of the spine and machine stitch together with a 1cm (³⁄₈in) seam allowance. Press the seams open.

{07} Join the inside panels
Hem one long edge on each of the cotton/linen fabric inside panels. With the right side of the album cover facing up, pin the inside panels in place, aligning the raw edges and sandwiching a piece of ribbon centrally at each side (for the ties). Machine stitch around the raw edges with a 6mm (¼in) seam allowance.

{08} Add the lining and finish
Pin the lining fabric on top with right sides facing, and machine stitch around the edge of the cover using a 1cm (³⁄₈in) seam allowance, leaving a 3cm (1¹⁄₈in) turning gap at the base of the spine. Snip the corners and turn the finished cover the right way out. Press, then slipstitch the opening closed by hand.

Sewing Story

This album was inspired by that most special of occasions, the wedding day. More specifically, I wanted to make something that was unique, personal and special, everything a wedding should be, and for the finished item itself to evoke memories of the celebration. *Emily Carlill*

Button-up A-line skirt

This cute button-up skirt is the ideal project to help you perfect your buttonhole technique. Designed to be worn just below the waist, it is made to your own measurements, so it will always fit perfectly. Made from a fine needlecord, it's perfect for those cooler autumn days, but you can change the fabric to match the season.

MATERIALS

1m (1⅛yd) of 150cm (60in) wide fabric in fabric of your choice

Six buttons

1m (1yd) of bias binding

Pencil and paper (brown or baking) for making pattern

Sewing machine and buttonhole foot (optional)

Fabric marking pencil

Scissors and seam ripper

Pins

Iron

Ruler and tape measure

SIZE

Custom fit to your measurements.

FEATURED TECHNIQUES

- Taking body measurements [p. 144]
- Machine-stitching techniques [p. 110]
- Seam finishes [p. 122]
- Sewing darts: single dart [p. 147]
- Machine-stitched hem [p. 125]
- Machine-sewn buttonhole [p. 132]
- Sewing on a button [p. 133]

DESIGNED BY SAMMY AND H

BEFORE YOU BEGIN

The button-up skirt shown is made from a lightweight cord, but you could use almost any fabric, from cotton lawn to denim or leatherette.

If you choose to make your skirt a little longer, or if you are using a nap or patterned fabric, you will need to buy a little more fabric to be sure all your pieces are cut in the same direction and for pattern matching.

If using a lightweight fabric, add a strip of interfacing to the front panels where the buttons and buttonholes will go.

A one-step buttonhole foot was used to sew the buttonholes but if your machine does not have this capability, review and practise the machine-sewn buttonhole technique (p. 132) on a spare scrap of your chosen fabric.

METHOD

{01} Draft your pattern and cut the back skirt panel

Taking a large piece of your chosen pattern paper, make the pattern piece to cut the back skirt panel. Start by measuring your hips at the widest part. Divide this measurement by 4, then add 1.5cm (⅝in). Draw a line (line A) the length of this measurement at the bottom of your paper sheet. At either end of this line, measure up 50cm (20in) to make a rectangle – the top of this rectangle marks the waistline (if you would like your skirt to be a little longer, add some length to this measurement).

Measure 6cm (2⅜in) from the bottom left-hand corner of the rectangle you have just made and make a mark (B), and extend line A to this point. Then measure 20cm (8in) down from the waistline and make a mark (C); draw a straight line from point C to B to make a triangle on the side of your skirt panel. Cut out around your marked outline to give you your back skirt panel pattern (see photo).

Fold your fabric in half with right sides facing and place the back skirt panel pattern with the long straight edge on the fold of the fabric and cut out the back panel.

{02} Draft the front skirt pattern and cut two front panels

To make the front skirt pattern, draw around the back skirt pattern onto your pattern paper and add an additional 7cm (2¾in) to the long straight edge and cut out (see photo). Use the front skirt pattern to cut two front skirt panels from your fabric.

{03} Sew the front panels to the back panel

Unfold the back panel and lay it out flat. Place the two front panels onto the back panel, with right sides together and matching up the

{01} waistline · C · A · B

{02} 7cm (2¾in) · add this piece

Once you have made your pattern pieces, you can use them to make this skirt over and over again, so store your pattern pieces in a folder with a photo of your finished skirt for reference.

side seams, and pin in place. Sew the side seams with a 1.5cm (⅝in) seam allowance, working from top to bottom. Press the seams open.

{04} Mark the darts

Fold the back panel in half to find the centre back, marking the centre point at the waist. Unfold and make a second mark half way between that centre back mark and each side seam to mark the position of the back darts. To mark the bottom point of each dart, measure 20cm (8in) down from the waistline and mark. Use these back panel markings to transfer the position for the front darts onto each of the front panels.

{04}

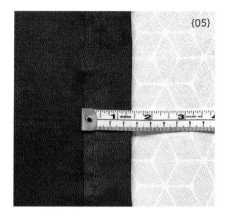

{05}

{05} Prepare the front panels for the button closure

Working now on the front panels of the skirt, fold under the long straight edge of the right-hand panel by 3.5cm (1⅜in) and sew it in place 3cm (1⅛in) from the fold.

Then fold under the long straight edge of the left-hand panel so that the front panels overlap by at least 3cm (1⅛in) in the centre. Pin the fold in place and sew rows of stitching 3.5cm (1⅜in) and 6mm (¼in) from the fold to create the buttonhole placket.

{06} Fit the skirt and sew the darts

Turn the skirt wrong side out and start to pin the front panels together at the centre working from the hem up. Carefully put on the skirt and finish pinning to the top . Pinch in the skirt at the waistline at the positions marked in step 4 to make the skirt fit your shape, and pin the darts in place

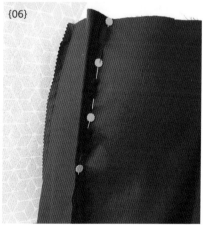

{06}

as shown above, with each dart finishing at the marks made 20cm (8in) down from the waistline.

Unpin the skirt at the centre front, then sew the darts you have pinned – two front, two back: press the darts to one side (see p. 147).

{07} Bind the waistline

Take the bias binding and place the raw edge to the waistline of the skirt, right sides together and pin it in place. Using the fold in the bias binding as a guide, stitch about 6mm (¼in) from the raw edge (07a).

Fold the bias binding all the way over to the inside of the skirt so that it is not visible from the right side of the skirt; pin it in place and topstitch as close to the bottom (raw) edge of the binding strip as you can (07b).

{07a}

{07b}

Sewing Story

My parents have always had a very practical influence on me. My mum has been sewing and altering clothes all her life, so I am lucky enough to have had a great teacher in her. *Heather Thomas*

{08} Hem the skirt

Fold up a small hem and sew it in place. You could use a double fold machine-stitched hem, or simply use pinking shears to trim away any excess from the hem to prevent the fabric from fraying.

{09} Make the buttonholes

Mark the position of your six buttonholes onto the buttonhole placket using a fabric marking pencil: place one at the waistband and one 7cm (2¾in) from the hem, and evenly spacing the other four in between.

Working your way down from top to bottom, sew the buttonholes horizontally . To cut through the sewn buttonholes, pop a pin in at the edge of the buttonhole placket (to stop you from going too far) and use a seam ripper to cut the fabric between the lines of stitching.

{10} Mark the button placement and sew on the buttons

Once you have cut your button-holes open, use them to mark the position of the buttons onto the right-hand front panel: taking care to align the front panels at the waistline and the hem, use a fabric marking pencil to draw the button positions through the buttonholes. Sew the buttons in place as marked.

{09}

Note

If you prefer not to work buttonholes, you could sew poppers down the front panels of your skirt instead. Then, to create the illusion of buttonholes, sew buttons onto the overlapping front panel.

New to sewing?

This section of the book contains all the step-by-step guidance you need to get started. So choose your fabric, thread up your machine and read on – in just a short while you'll be stitching with confidence.

Seasoned pro?

If you've already completed a few sewing projects, use this section to build up your skills. Packed with hints, tips and techniques, it will springboard you into developing your sewing skills. Before long, your humble home will be bursting at the seams with your creations, and friends will be admiring your custom-made clothes.

Techniques

Sewing equipment

{ To begin your sewing adventures, you will need a few pieces of essential equipment. Start by purchasing the nuts and bolts: needles and pins, a tape measure, your choice of marking tools, fabric shears, a seam ripper, and a sewing machine, of course.

MEASURING AND MARKING TOOLS

You probably have perfectly adequate tools for measuring and marking in your sewing box or on your desk, but a few special purchases could make your life a little easier.

Note

You may also find the following items useful for making the self-drafted patterns for the sundress and skirt on pp. 46 and 84, although neither is essential: dressmaking pattern cutting paper is printed with markings, usually dots and crosses, and the space between markings is exactly 1 inch for the accurate transfer of measurements; a French curve is used to draw shaped or curved areas, such as armholes and necklines.

MEASURING TOOLS

Accurate measuring is very important for most sewing projects. Whichever tool you choose to use for the job, remember the golden rule: take every measurement at least twice.

Tape measure: A flexible tape measure is essential to take measurements of the body or any three-dimensional item, but avoid fabric tapes as these can stretch over time.

Retractable metal tape measure: Useful for measuring up windows for curtains or similar tasks.

Adjustable ruler: A fold-out wooden ruler that extends to quite a length and is also reasonably stiff is handy for measuring areas where a metal tape measure might buckle, such as windows or beneath furniture.

Seam gauge: A small metal ruler with sliding marker is useful for achieving seams of an even depth; it's particularly good for measuring accurate widths of borders on quilts.

Metal ruler: A metal ruler makes a reliable cutting guide that can withstand a knife blade without being damaged.

Plastic ruler: The advantage of a plastic ruler is that it is transparent, allowing you to see everything as you work; do not use it as a cutting guide, however, as sharp tools will damage its edge.

MARKING TOOLS

When transferring markings – pattern-matching symbols or embroidery designs, for example – there are many choices available to you. Your aim is to make a visible mark on the fabric that will not show on the finished project. Test your choice on both the right and wrong side of the fabric to determine if it is suitable.

Water-soluble marker: Sponging with water or washing removes the marks made with this tool, so it may not be suitable for fabrics that must be dry cleaned or that are difficult to wash.

Air-soluble marker: Marks made by this tool will slowly fade over time, so it may not be suitable for use on a project that will take a long time to complete.

Chalk pencil/tailor's pencil: The chalk is available in several colours and the pencil often has a stiff brush at one end for removing marks when no longer required.

Tailor's chalk: Also called dressmaker's chalk, this is available in a range of colours and is useful for creating different weights of line. Marks can be brushed away easily.

Chalk wheel: An easy-to-use dispenser that can be refilled with different colours of chalk powder, so you can choose a colour that will show up well on your fabric.

Tracing wheel: Dressmaker's carbon is placed between the pattern and the fabric, then the tracing wheel is run along the lines of the design to transfer a dotted outline to the fabric. This is one of the quickest ways to transfer continuous lines, but as the marks may be difficult to remove, it is best used for designs that will be hidden by stitching.

CUTTING TOOLS

Achieving a clean-cut edge is crucial if you want professional-looking results. Choose the right cutting tool for the job and make sure your sewing scissors are never used for anything else!

Thread/embroidery scissors: A small pair of scissors with sharp points is ideal for snipping thread, for fine detail fabric cutting, and to snip into awkward corners. For thread only, special thread clippers are ideal for both right- and left-handed people.

Fabric scissors or dressmaker's shears: Any scissors used for cutting fabric must be very sharp with good long blades. Choose a pair that sits comfortably in your hand. Special

dressmaker's shears have one handle at an angle to the blades. This allows the blade to slide along the work surface in a more horizontal position, keeping the fabric flat to the surface for more accurate cutting.

General/paper scissors: A spare pair of ordinary scissors is useful for cutting paper patterns and synthetic wadding, and for other general cutting work.

Pinking shears: These shears have notched blades so they cut a zigzag line. They are useful to trim raw seam edges to help prevent fraying and to create a decorative edge on non-fraying fabric.

Seam ripper: This is an invaluable tool with a sharp prong to push into stitches and a tiny sharp blade to

slice through thread. It can be used to unpick seams quickly and to cut the slit for machine-stitched buttonholes.

Quilter's rule: A favourite tool of many a quilter, this is an acrylic ruler marked with a grid of squares. It is useful for cutting small pieces of fabric for patchwork.

Rotary cutter: A cutter with a circular wheel that makes a continuous cut and can slice through several layers of fabric at a time. It is most often used to cut out numerous identical shapes for patchwork. When using a rotary cutter, always protect your work surface with a cutting mat; it is self-healing, so it can be cut into many times without showing a mark.

SEWING MACHINE

If you are lucky, you may be able to borrow a friend's machine to get you started, but it won't be long before you will want to invest in your own, and you may be surprised at how affordable they can be.

WHICH MACHINE?

There are many different types of sewing machine available on the market, ranging from basic designs with only a small selection of stitches to computerised models that can automatically stitch detailed embroidery designs from a picture or photograph. Below are a few examples of what is on offer. As a general rule, the more stitches and functions a machine has, the more expensive it will be. However, there is very little point in paying extra for features you just won't use. Visit a showroom and try out different machines and take full advantage of any professional instruction that may be offered.

The instruction book will explain your specific machine, but most share some common features. For more about this, see pp. 105–107.

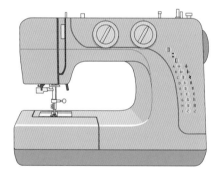

A budget electric machine has no fancy extras so it is very simple to operate. It will only have a small range of pre-set stitches and may not have some functions, such as the option to adjust the stitch width; however, it will be fine for basic sewing.

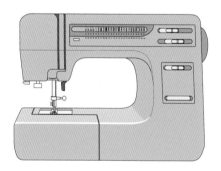

A mid-range electric machine will have a wider range of pre-set stitches, including a one-step automatic buttonhole, the ability to adjust stitch width as well as length, and extra functions, such as adjustable foot pressure. Check which extra functions you need before making a final decision between different models.

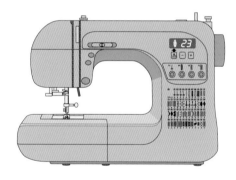

A basic computerised machine, as seen here, will have a wide range of pre-set stitches, including several buttonhole designs, and stitch width and length can be used as pre-set or adjusted to create special effects. A higher-specification computerised machine will have hundreds of pre-set stitches, as well as extra functions, such as the ability to create and memorise a stitch sequence.

PINNING EQUIPMENT

Pinning holds the pattern to the fabric when cutting, but it is also an effective way to hold layers of fabric together when machine stitching.

Pins: Plain steel pins are ideal for most fabrics and for very delicate fabrics an extra-fine version is available. Extra-long pins are available for when you need to hold several thick layers together, such as in quiltmaking.

Glass-headed pins: Pins with a large coloured head are often easier to spot when you come to remove them – choose glass-headed rather than plastic, which might melt if inadvertently ironed over.

Pin cushion: You can keep your pins in a plastic box – a tin may make them go rusty – but a pin cushion saves having to open a box when you need a pin in a hurry.

HAND-SEWING EQUIPMENT

Hand stitching is an essential part of both dressmaking and many home furnishing projects. High-quality professional items are almost always finished by hand, even if much of the basic sewing has been done by machine. So, equip yourself with a few essentials.

HAND-SEWING NEEDLES

Illustrated below right are, from left to right:

Sharps: These ordinary sewing needles are available in several sizes.

Darner: A long needle used for darning and tacking.

Large-eye embroidery: For thicker embroidery yarn.

Small-eye embroidery: For fine embroidery yarn.

Tapestry: With a large eye for canvas embroidery; also useful for threading thin elastic or ribbon.

Needle threader: Push the wire loop through the needle eye, slide the thread end through the loop and pull it back through the eye, taking the thread with it.

THREAD

Thread comes in a range of colours and fibres – both natural and synthetic. It also comes in different thicknesses for a variety of purposes, from tacking to embroidery. Thicker threads are normally used for techniques like topstitching, where the stitches are visible as part of the design.

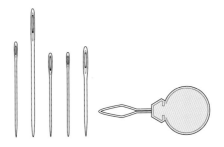

Note

Tacking thread is a fine cotton thread that comes in a limited range of colours and is made to break for easy and swift removal of tacking (long running) stitches when they are no longer needed to temporarily hold layers of fabric together once the fabric layers have been permanently sewn together.

PRESSING EQUIPMENT

As well as pressing the finished item, you will often need to press your work at regular intervals throughout the sewing process – pressing seams open or the folds of a hem, for instance. You can use your regular ironing surface and steam iron for this, but there are also a couple of additional pieces of equipment that you may find useful.

Steam iron: An ordinary household steam iron is fine, but be careful not to get water on 'dry clean only' fabrics, as it may leave marks that are difficult to remove.

Pressing cloth: Use to avoid marking delicate items or wool.

Tailor's ham: A rounded, three-dimensional shape, the tailor's ham is useful for pressing curved seams and awkward shapes.

Ironing board: If you are working on a large project or plan to do a lot of sewing, it makes sense to keep an ironing board close to your sewing work space.

Sleeveboard: Put simply, this is a smaller, narrower ironing board that sits on top of the main board or on a tabletop. It is used to press narrow tubes of fabric, such as sleeves.

PRESSING TECHNIQUES

Pressing is essential to achieve neat seams and hems to give your projects a neat finish. You should use only the tip of the iron and work quite lightly. Do not press over bulky areas, such as zips and pockets.

Note

To fingerpress, place the piece on a hard surface, wrong side upward, and run your finger along the seam to press it flat. This technique is not suitable for fabrics that will stretch or fray easily.

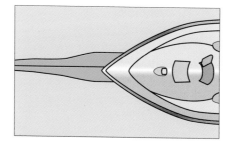

FLAT SEAMS
Remove any pins and tacking, and with the wrong side facing upward, open out the seam. Run the tip of the iron along the seam to press it flat.

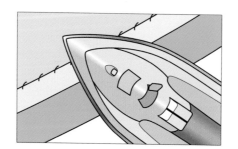

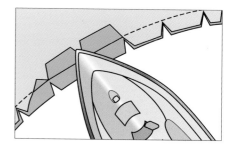

CLIPPED SEAMS
Place the piece flat on the ironing board, wrong side upward, and the seam allowances lying together. Use the point of the iron to press back the top layer of the seam allowance.

HEMS
Press hems from the fold towards the stitching, with the wrong side uppermost, to avoid the edge of the hem showing on the right side.

Stitching by hand

Although many projects can be made almost entirely on the sewing machine, there will almost certainly be some hand stitching required. So, whether you are stitching by hand to join pieces together or to decorate a project, it's time to learn the stitches you'll need to complete the projects in this book.

UTILITY STITCHES

The basic hand-sewn stitches are very easy to do. Always sew with a thread no more than 60cm (24in) in length – a longer thread will weaken and tangle as it is repeatedly pulled through the fabric. Most hand sewing will be done with a single thread, but for added security you can use a double thread to sew on buttons or other fasteners.

QUICK KNOTTING

The most common method to secure a length of thread before you begin stitching is to make a knot at the end. Hold the threaded needle in your right hand, pressing against the eye so the thread cannot slip out. Take the other end of the thread in your left hand and use your right hand to bring the thread right around the tip of the index finger to cross over the thread end. Use your left thumb to roll the loop off your finger into a knot.

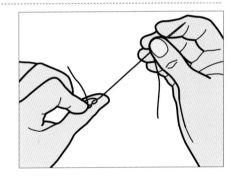

FINISHING OFF

Used at the end of a row of stitching or when the thread has run out: take a small stitch on the wrong side of the fabric, wrap the thread several times around the point of the needle, then pull the needle through the wrapped threads to form a knot close to the surface of the fabric.

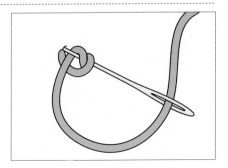

RUNNING STITCH

A long running stitch is used to join layers of fabric together temporarily to prevent slipping as seams are stitched and this is referred to as tacking. Running stitch is also required for gathering. But this essential utility stitch can also be worked decoratively for hand-embroidered details.

To work running stitch, take the needle in and out of the fabric several times, picking up a small stitch through all the layers each time. Pull the thread through gently until it is taut, but don't pull it so tight that the fabric puckers up. Continue to make a row of even stitches, with the stitches on the wrong side matching those on the right.

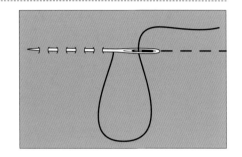

BACKSTITCH

Backstitch creates a row of stitches set end-to-end and looking from the right side like machine stitching, but with the end of each stitch overlapping the next on the wrong side. It is ideal for mending and to hand stitch short seams securely.

To work backstitch, bring the needle through the fabric then insert it a short distance behind where it came out and bring it up through the fabric again the same distance ahead. Each subsequent stitch begins at the end of the previous stitch and all the stitches should be the same size.

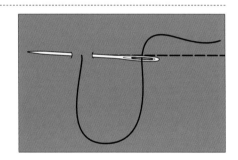

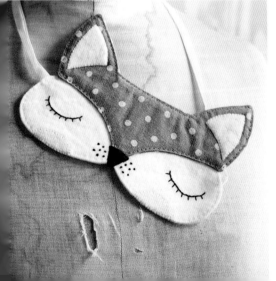

WHIPSTITCH

Also known as overcasting or oversewing, whipstitch is a row of diagonal hand stitching done over raw edges, particularly of a seam, to prevent fraying or unravelling. For a neater finish, fold the raw edges before oversewing them together.

The foxy sleep mask (p. 70) was hand stitched using a neat backstitch.

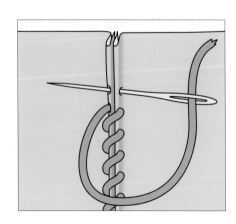

SLIPSTITCH

This almost invisible stitch is used to join two folded edges together or to secure a folded edge to a flat piece of fabric, when hemming for example.

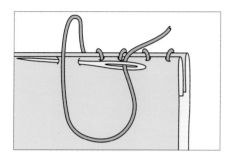

TO JOIN TWO FOLDED EDGES TOGETHER

Lay the pieces one on top of the other, folded edge to folded edge, and bring the needle through the folded edge of the bottom piece from the back so the knotted end is secured inside the fold. Take a tiny stitch through the edge of the top fold, then go back into the top layer of the bottom piece of fabric and slide the needle a little way along inside the fold to come out again on the edge. Continue in this way until the seam is complete.

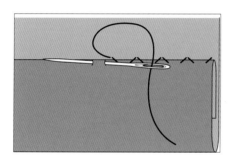

TO SECURE A FOLDED EDGE TO A FLAT PIECE OF FABRIC

Bring the needle up through the folded edge of one side, take a tiny stitch through just one or two threads in the opposite (flat) layer of fabric, then insert the needle back into the fold of the first layer. Slide the needle along inside the fold a short way, and then repeat the sequence – the stitches should be almost invisible on both the right and the wrong side of the fabric layers.

HEMMING STITCH

Secure the end of the thread inside the hem by taking a tiny stitch through a single layer of the hem allowance on the wrong side. Bring the needle through to the right side near the top edge of the hem allowance and then take a tiny, inconspicuous stitch through a couple of threads of the main fabric just above. Try not to let this stitch show on the right side of the item. Take the needle diagonally down between the layers of fabric and up through to the right side a little further along the hem. Continue in this way, spacing the stitches around 6mm (¼in) apart.

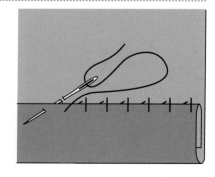

DECORATIVE STITCHES

By mastering just a few basic techniques you can embellish your projects with a little creative stitchery. The running stitch and backstitch, introduced in the utility stitches section, can also be used decoratively and there are a handful more you'll need to learn to make the featured projects, including chain stitch and French knots.

TRANSFERRING EMBROIDERY DESIGNS

Once you have enlarged your embroidery design to actual size using a photocopier or scanner, transfer it to your fabric using one of these methods.

TRANSFER PENCIL OR PEN TRACING METHOD

Use a transfer pencil or pen to go over the reverse of a tracing of the embroidery design; place the paper, transfer-pencil side down, on the right side of the fabric and press, holding the iron perfectly still (to avoid blurring) for a count of 10.

LIGHT-BOX METHOD

Tape the photocopied design to a light-box (or a bright window). Tape your fabric on top of the photocopy. Trace the design onto your fabric using a soft pencil or water-soluble marker for example, to make an outline that will be hidden by your stitching or which is easy to remove once the embroidery is complete.

Working the bird embroidery on the peg bag (p. 21).

USING AN EMBROIDERY HOOP

To help ensure even embroidery, it can really help to keep the fabric taut during stitching by using an embroidery hoop, for example. Available in a variety of sizes, these consist of two circles of wood (or plastic), one inside the other, with a tension screw on the outer circle. Always remember to remove the hoop at the end of a stitching session as it can distort the fabric.

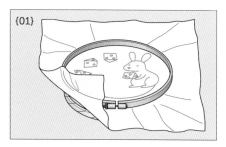

{01}

Bind the smaller ring with cloth tape, then place it under the fabric. Place the larger ring over the fabric, centring the image.

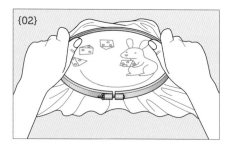

{02}

Slightly open the screw on the larger ring and push down. Pull the fabric edges to make sure it is taut, and tighten the screw.

STARTING THREAD

You should never start your stitching with a knot at the back of your first stitch, as this will result in unsightly bumps. For neat results, use one of the following methods.

OVERSTITCHING

Pull a threaded needle through the fabric from the back to the front leaving a tail at the back 4cm (1½in) long. Begin stitching, holding this thread at the back of the work until it is secured by your stitches. Trim off excess thread.

USING A KNOT

Make a knot at the end of the thread and take the needle down on the front of the fabric. (Working left to right, position knot 4cm/1½in to right of first stitch.) Work stitches over thread at the back. When secure, cut off the knot and pull the thread tail to the back.

AWAY WASTE KNOT

Make a knot at the end of the thread and take the needle down on the front of the fabric, about 15cm (6in) away from the stitching area. To finish, clip knot and weave the thread tail into the back of the work.

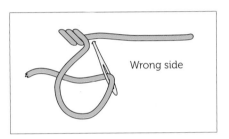

Wrong side

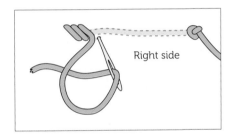

Right side

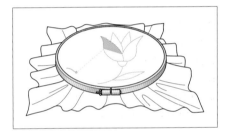

FINISHING OFF THREAD

Take the needle through to the back of the fabric and weave it in and out of three or four adjacent stitches. Pull the thread through the stitches gently.

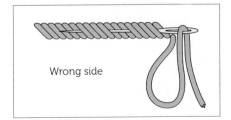

Wrong side

Embroidery details can bring personality to your finished pieces, as can be seen on the dapper bear pyjama case (p. 64).

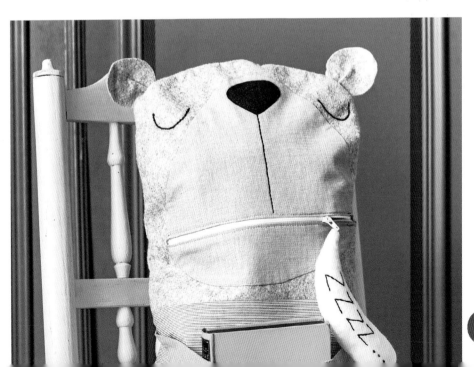

CHAIN STITCH

Chain stitch is a member of the looped stitch family and it is most often used as an outline stitch. It is important to keep an even tension so that the chain stitch loops appear consistently open or round. Fine outlines can be created and curved shapes can be intricately followed with this stitch.

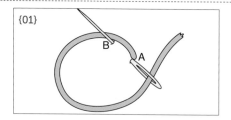

{01}

Come up at A. Go down to left of A, coming up at B. Loop thread under needle point from right to left.

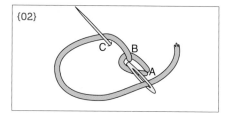

{02}

Pull thread through. Go down to left of B, inserting through loop, and come up at C. Loop thread as in step 1. Aim for an even row of equally sized stitches.

Note

To work looped stitches, use your non-stitching thumb to hold and guide the thread around the needle as you work. This will help prevent the thread from tangling or knotting.

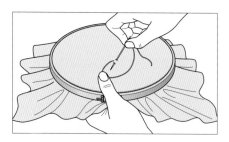

DETACHED CHAIN STITCH

This detached chain stitch variation is worked in exactly the same way as basic chain stitch, except that each stitch is finished individually and secured to the fabric with a small straight stitch at the top of the loop. Stitches can be worked individually to create leaves, or in circles for flowers.

To work a detached chain stitch start by following step 1 above. Pull through and make a small stitch to anchor the

loop. Work five (or more) detached chain stitches in a circle to create a flower shape.

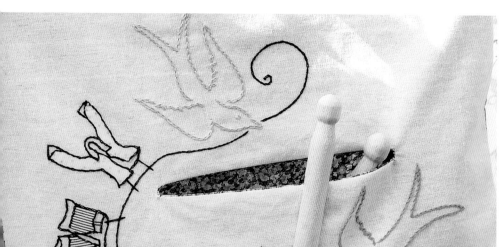

Chain stitch was used for the embroidery detailing on the peg bag (p. 20): the birds were stitched using two strands of embroidery thread in the needle and the washing line and clothes' outlines with just one strand.

BUTTONHOLE AND BLANKET STITCH

Buttonhole stitches are placed very close together to form a tight line. Blanket stitches are worked the same way, except space is left between each vertical stitch. To work an attractive buttonhole stitch, you are aiming to keep the tops of the stitches level. Before beginning, draw guidelines on your fabric.

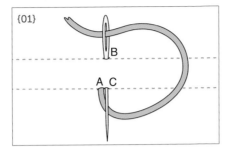

Come up at A, go down at B, come up at C, just to immediate right of A. Carry thread under needle point from left to right. Pull thread through.

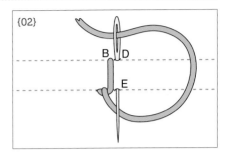

Go down at D (just to immediate right of B). Come up at E, keeping thread under the tip of the needle.

Note

Buttonhole stitch makes a firm, strong edge finish and can be used, worked over waxed thread or cord, to stitch buttonholes by hand.

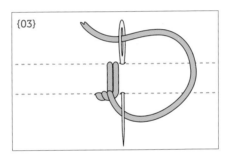

Continue in this way along row, keeping all stitches even and close together as shown.

A neat blanket stitch is worked to hold the front and the back of the wedding charms together (p. 6).

SATIN STITCH

Satin stitch is made up of simple straight stitches laid close together in parallel lines to create a solid yet smooth filling stitch. It can be used to fill motifs of all shapes. For the best results, stretch your fabric in a hoop and place stitches next to each other to prevent the background fabric from showing through.

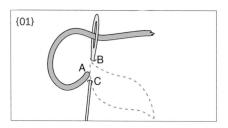

{01}

Come up at A, go down at B, come up at C. Pull thread through gently, ready for next stitch.

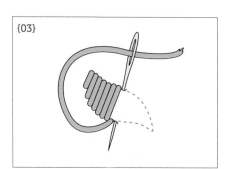

{02}

Placing stitches close together, go down at D and come up at E. Follow exact guidelines of motif for even edge.

Continue to fill motif, keeping an even tension so that the surface remains smooth.

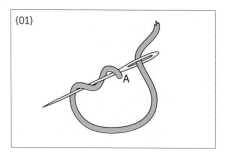

{03}

FRENCH KNOTS

The French knot is a compact raised stitch resembling a bead lying on its side. It can be used individually for details such as eyes, or in clusters as seen on the foxy sleep mask (see p. 70). Achieving the perfect French knot requires some practise.

Note

Wrap the thread around the needle in a clockwise or anti-clockwise direction, but be consistent. Increase the knot size by using more strands of thread, using a heavier thread or increasing the number of wraps.

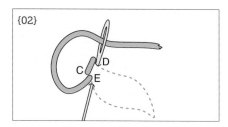

{01}

Come up at A and wrap thread around needle once in anti-clockwise direction. Wrap thread around needle a second time in same direction, keeping needle away from fabric.

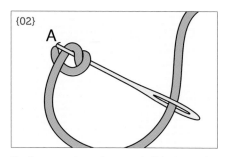

{02}

Push wraps together and slide to end of needle. Go down close to start point, pulling thread through to form the knot.

Using a sewing machine

New to machine stitching? This chapter has all the information you need to get started with confidence, including a guided tour of a sewing machine with details of the main working parts and what they do. There's also a beginner's guide to machine-stitching techniques.

A PLACE TO SEW

Find somewhere to set up your machine so that you will be comfortable while working, choosing a place with as much natural light as possible. Make sure you have all the equipment you will need close at hand before you begin your project.

GOOD POSTURE

When working at the sewing machine for long periods, your forearms should be at a 90-degree angle to your body and the sewing bed should be at the same level as the bottom of your elbows. To achieve this you might need a higher chair or a lower table than normal. Your wrists should be resting about midway between your waist and chest. To avoid neck or back strain and to allow ease of movement, a chair with a straight back and no arms is best.

Take some time to be sure you are comfortable because working in an awkward position for long periods will soon lead to backache.

SEWING MACHINE FEATURES

This section introduces the basic functions that are common to most machines, but it's always worth checking your manual.

FREE ARM

If a machine has a free-arm facility, (see 14 overleaf), it is usually brought into use by detaching a piece on the base to leave the arm protruding, so sleeves and trouser legs can then be threaded on for easier stitching.

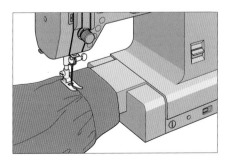

FRONT

1 Foot pressure dial: To adjust foot pressure when sewing lightweight or heavyweight fabrics or bulky layers; however, a machine with automatic foot pressure will be adequate for the average sewing project.

2 Thread take-up lever: Moves up and down with the needle and controls the amount of thread needed for stitching.

3 Bobbin thread guide with tension disc: To take the thread from the spool to the bobbin winding spindle. This guide has a tension disc so the bobbin thread is wound tightly.

4 Speed control: This enables you to limit the maximum stitching speed for more even stitching.

5 Thread guides: There are several of these along the threading run to take the thread in the right direction.

6 Bobbin winder spindle: Used when filling up the bobbin with thread.

7 Stitch width dial: Controls the distance the needle moves from side to side when sewing zigzag or other decorative stitches.

8 Stitch length dial: For adjusting the length of your stitches – a machine that allows a good range of stitch lengths will be more versatile.

9 Stitch selector dial: Used to select the machine's built-in stitches.

10 Reverse stitch lever: Allows you to sew in reverse. On some models reverse stitch is selected by turning the stitch length dial (see 8) to a minus number.

11 Drop feed lever: Lowers the feed dog below the needle plate to put it out of action when free-motion sewing. Alternatively, it may be possible to temporarily fix a plate over the feed dog. For more on this, see pp. 108 and 141.

12 Knee lifter socket: Where the knee lifter (if one is provided) plugs in. A knee lifter is a long bar with a bend that slots into the front of a machine and extends down next to the knee. It allows you to lift and lower the presser foot with your knee, so leaving both hands free to manipulate the fabric.

13 Hook cover release button: Releases the hook cover plate to access the bobbin

14 Flat bed: A large flat sewing area. On some machines part of this may detach to reveal the free arm.

15 Hook cover plate: Covers the bobbin in its casing. (The bobbin holds the lower thread, see p. 108.)

16 Needle plate: Marked with common seam allowances as a guide to accurate sewing.

17 Thread cutter: For cutting the needle thread.

18 Tension dial: Used to adjust the tension of the needle thread for a perfectly balanced stitch.

BACK

19 Foot control socket: Connect the plug here for the foot pedal that controls the stitching speed.

20 Power switch: Turns the power and the machine's built-in sewing light on or off.

21 Hand wheel: Turning the hand wheel raises and lowers the needle. Always turn the hand wheel counter-clockwise.

22 Thread cutter: Used to cut the bobbin thread when the bobbin is fully wound.

23 Bobbin winder stopper: This is pushed against the bobbin when winding begins. When the bobbin is full it pops back and stops the bobbin winding mechanism.

24 Carrying handle: Always carry the machine by its handle.

25 Thread spool pins: These hold the thread for the needle and can be set vertically or horizontally.

26 Presser foot lifting lever: Lift to slide the fabric beneath, or when changing the presser foot. For more detail, see p. 109.

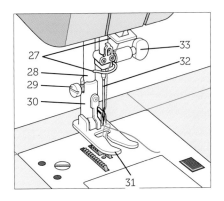

PRESSER FOOT DETAIL

27 Thread guides: Take the needle thread towards the eye of the needle.

28 Presser bar: The foot holder clips around this, held in place by the thumbscrew.

29 Presser foot thumbscrew: Releases the entire presser foot holder.

30 Presser foot holder: Clips onto the presser bar – on some machines the foot and the foot holder are all one piece.

31 Presser foot: Holds the fabric firmly against the needle plate and feed dog so that the stitches form properly.

32 Needle: The needle takes the upper thread through the fabric and down through the needle plate.

33 Needle clamp screw: Loosen to remove a needle; tighten to secure a needle in position.

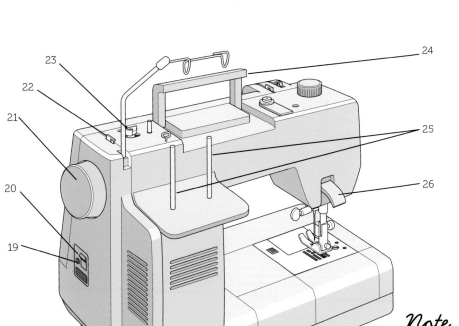

Note

Some options will vary across different makes and models and the actual location and configuration of some of these features may vary, depending on the make and model of your machine

HOW A SEWING MACHINE WORKS

Most modern domestic sewing machines perform lockstitch, in which one thread comes down through the needle and a second thread comes up from the bobbin. The needle (upper) thread and bobbin (lower) thread each stay on their own side of the fabric, but if the tension is correct, they interlock in the middle of the layers of fabric, creating a secure stitch that looks the same on both sides (for more on thread tension, see p. 112).

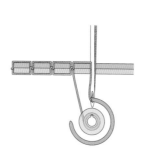

The needle takes a loop of thread through the fabric and down through the hole in the needle plate.

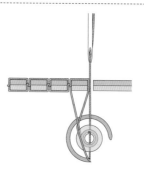

The loop of thread from the needle is caught by a rotary hook and looped around the thread from the bobbin.

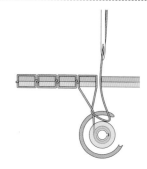

The rotary hook finishes its circular rotation, releasing the needle thread so that it pulls the bobbin thread up into the fabric.

FABRIC FEED

The fabric is normally fed through the sewing machine by the drop feed mechanism. When the needle moves upwards and withdraws from the fabric, the feed dog comes up through slots in the needle plate and the serrated top surface grips the material, which is held firmly against it by the presser foot. The feed dog moves horizontally backwards, so the fabric is dragged backwards into position for the next stitch. The feed dog is then lowered again and returns to its original position while the needle makes its next pass through the fabric.

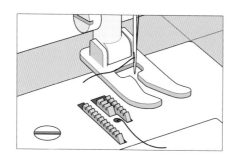

The feed dog comes up though slots in the needle plate and the serrated top surface grips the material.

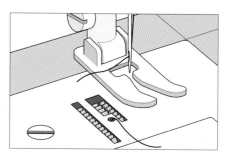

The feed dog is then lowered and returns to its original position

Note

The feed dog automatically feeds the fabric under the presser foot as you stitch. By dropping the feed dog – the little 'teeth' that come up into the needle plate as you sew to pull the fabric through – or by using a raised needle plate (see p. 141), you put yourself firmly in control. For free-motion work you need to be able to move the fabric around under the needle at will, and this is achieved by putting the feed dog out of action, either by dropping it or by covering it with a plate.

PRESSER FEET

The presser foot is a shaped piece of metal or plastic with a hole through which the needle stitches. It sits below the needle and holds the fabric securely against the feed dog as the machine stitches. It can be raised when you want to slide the fabric under the needle, then lowered again to hold the fabric against the needle plate.

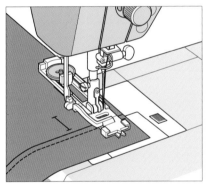

Automatic buttonhole foot

TYPES OF PRESSER FEET

Presser feet can easily be changed and there are many different types of foot available for different sewing tasks. Your sewing machine will almost certainly come with a few basic presser feet – usually a standard or zigzag foot, a zipper foot and maybe a buttonhole foot – and these will be all that you need to begin with, but as your skills develop you might want to invest in some special feet. A few examples are shown below but it is worth taking the time to explore what is available for your sewing machine model.

Automatic buttonhole foot: This has a special attachment that holds the button and sizes the buttonhole automatically to fit.

Rolled (or narrow) hem foot: This has a special curled piece of metal at the front, which turns the edge of light and medium-weight fabrics under to create a double folded hem as you stitch. Rolled hem feet come in several sizes to create hems from 1mm (1/32in) to 6mm (1/4in) wide.

Darning foot: Also known as the quilting, embroidery or appliqué foot, this has a small round or C-shaped end so very little of the stitching area is obscured. It is often used with the feed dog disengaged for greater control of stitching direction.

Zipper foot: This narrow foot slides down the side of the zip teeth instead of straddling them. It is also useful for inserting piping into a seam.

Note

Most new machines come with a basic package of accessories including two or three extra feet. Check the manufacturer's website for details of specialised parts.

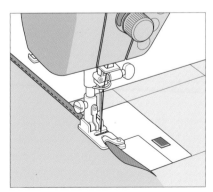

Rolled hem foot

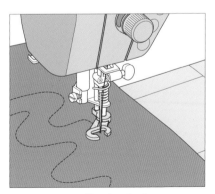

Darning foot

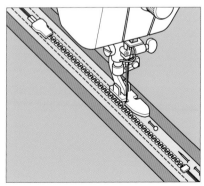

Zipper foot

MACHINE-STITCHING TECHNIQUES

If you are new to sewing with a machine, spend some time getting used to stitching with it before beginning work on a project. The first few techniques covered here are the real basics of machine stitching. Practise sewing on easy-to-sew calico and then explore working on other fabrics.

STARTING STITCHING

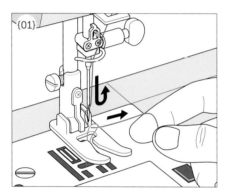

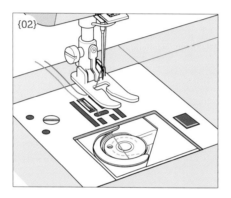

Make sure the needle and bobbin are threaded correctly. With the presser foot raised, take hold of the end of the needle thread and grip it firmly between finger and thumb. Turn the hand wheel once, so the needle goes down through the needle plate and back up again. The upper (needle) thread will catch the lower (bobbin) thread and pull a loop of it back up through the needle plate. Pull gently on the needle thread to raise the loop upwards until you can get hold of it.

Pull the loop gently to bring the loose end of the bobbin thread through to the top (you can check that the thread of the bobbin is passing diagonally across the top of the bobbin, but close the panel again). Take the needle thread under the presser foot and feed both thread ends to the back.

(03) Make sure the needle and bobbin threads are pulled under and behind, or to the side, of the raised presser foot. Place the fabric under the presser foot so that the bulk of the fabric is to the left of the presser foot. Turn the hand wheel to lower the needle into the fabric. Lower the presser foot and begin stitching, starting off slowly.

Note

Good-quality stitching is dependent on having the correct needle, thread, tension and stitch length for the fabric you are using. Always test-stitch on a scrap of the actual fabric before you begin any project.

WHERE TO POSITION YOUR HANDS

As you continue to stitch, your hands should be positioned on either side of the needle so that you can guide the fabric through the machine easily. Keep your fingers clear of the needle while sewing.

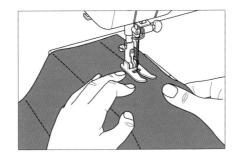

GUIDING THE FABRIC THROUGH THE MACHINE

Keep the bulk of the material to the left of the needle. Use your hands to steer the fabric in the right direction and to keep the edge aligned with the seam allowance guide (see below). Don't pull or push the fabric to move it through the machine – let the feed dog move it at the correct pace to match the action of the needle. Your hands should just be guiding the fabric into the machine and keeping it straight. It will take practice to stitch at a steady speed while steering the material under the needle. If your machine has a speed limiter function, it can help you to control your pace as you get to grips with the machine-stitching technique.

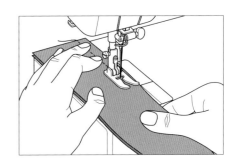

USING THE SEAM ALLOWANCE GUIDE

To keep seam allowances even, look for lines on the needle plate that indicate common seam allowances – the space between the edge of the fabric and the stitching line. In most cases the seam allowance will be 1.5cm (⅝in), 1cm (⅜in), or 6mm (¼in). If you want to use an unusual seam allowance width, you can mark it yourself with masking tape.

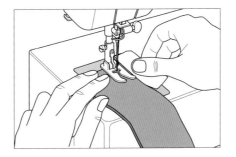

Note

Try to avoid sewing with an almost empty bobbin or spool of thread – the thread may not feed evenly, which will cause stitching problems.

SECURING THE THREAD ENDS

Backstitch, the reverse stitch on the sewing machine, is used to reinforce the stitching at the beginning and end of a seam to prevent the threads pulling loose. Start off around 1.5cm (⅝in) from the beginning of the seam and reverse stitch back to the edge, then stitch forward as normal. At the end, finish by reversing back along the stitching line for around 1.5cm (⅝in).

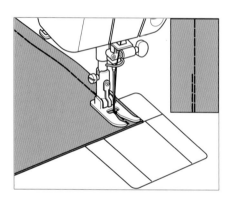

TURNING A CORNER

To achieve a neat, sharp turn in a seam when it needs to go around a corner, stitch to the exact point at which you need to turn. Leaving the needle down in the fabric, lift the presser foot.

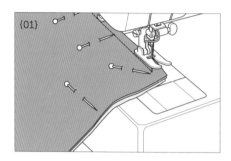

Swivel the work around on the needle – being careful not to pull on the needle – so that you are stitching in the new direction. Lower the presser foot, then begin stitching again.

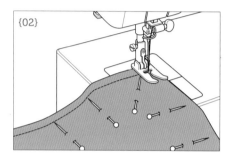

THREAD TENSION

To test the tension is correct, stitch a seam on a scrap of the fabric you will be using for your project.

BALANCED STITCH

If the tension is the same on both top and bottom threads, the stitch is perfectly balanced, so the two threads interlink in the middle of the layers of fabric. The line of stitching will look exactly the same on both sides.

TOP THREAD TOO LOOSE

If the bottom thread is tighter than the top thread, the bottom thread will lie in a line with loops of the top thread showing over the top. Tighten the top thread tension to correct this. Consult your sewing machine manual.

TOP THREAD TOO TIGHT

If the top thread is tighter than the bottom thread, the top thread will lie in a line with loops of the bottom thread showing over the top. Loosen the top thread tension to correct this. Consult your sewing machine manual.

STITCH GLOSSARY

These are your basic machine stitches. Take the time to try them out on different weights and types of fabric before starting work on a specific project. For more on fabric types, see pp. 114–117.

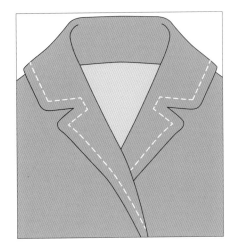

TOPSTITCHING

An extra line of stitching made parallel to a finished edge, topstitching is usually done in contrasting thread as a decorative feature. It may also be used to attach items such as patch pockets or to keep seam allowances flat. To make topstitching more pronounced, slightly loosen the top thread tension. If the stitching is being done through several layers, it may also be necessary to adjust the foot pressure.

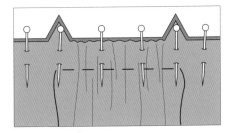

EASESTITCHING

Easestitching is used to reduce the length of an edge so it can be joined to a slightly shorter edge without visible folds or gathers. Stitch a single line between the points to be eased with the stitch length at its longest setting. Pin the two edges together at the ends, then pull the bobbin thread on the stitching to distribute the fullness of the edge evenly. Stitch the seam with the eased edge on top and the flat edge below.

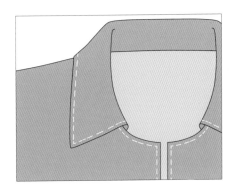

EDGESTITCHING

A line of stitching made approximately 3mm (⅛in) from a seamline or foldline or very close to a finished edge to keep the edge crisp. It is usually done in thread to match the fabric.

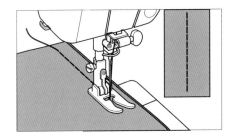

STRAIGHT STITCH

This is the most basic type of machine stitching possible. For most straight stitching on seams, the stitch length on the machine should be set at around 2–3. When using straight stitching for decorative stitching, try out the stitch length on a scrap of the actual fabric you will be using to select the best stitch length for the effect you want to achieve.

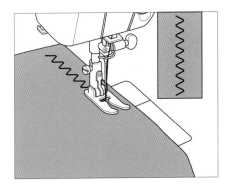

ZIGZAG

Zigzag stitch is used to finish raw edges and to stitch seams that need to have some give, such as for knit fabrics. The stitch width controls the width of the line of zigzag; the stitch length controls how tightly together the stitches are.

Working with fabric

It is one thing to practise machine-stitching techniques on calico but quite another when you come to work on other fabrics. It helps to understand a little about fabric structure and the challenges of working with certain fabrics before you begin.

FABRIC STRUCTURE

Fabric can be woven, knitted or nonwoven and each type has different characteristics, strengths and weaknesses.

WOVEN FABRICS

All woven fabrics are made up of two sets of yarn – the warp and the weft. The warp runs lengthwise in the loom and is sometimes also known as the floating yarn/threads. The weft runs widthwise at right angles to the warp and is sometimes known as the filling yarn, the filler or the woof. Woven fabrics can be created with different patterns by using warp and weft yarns in different sequences.

The selvage is the border that runs lengthwise down both edges of a length of woven fabric. Since it is often woven more tightly than the main fabric to stop the edges fraying the selvage may pucker when the fabric is cleaned, so generally it is cut away and discarded for sewing projects. Straight, or lengthwise, grain refers to the threads that are parallel to the selvage, while the crosswise grain refers to the threads that run across the fabric between the two selvages. The lengthwise and widthwise direction – or grain – of a woven fabric is firm, so fabric has very little give in these directions, although pattern pieces are usually laid out along the lengthwise grain

because it is most stable. However, if pulled diagonally – or on the bias – the fabric will stretch. True bias is at a 45-degree angle to the selvage and has the greatest stretch. Edges cut on the bias tend to stretch out of shape easily so seams must be stitched with care. In dressmaking, however, fabric is often cut and stitched on the bias as it results in clothes that drape and move with the body.

KNITTED FABRICS

All knitted fabrics are constructed using one set of yarn running in the same direction – looping the yarn around itself holds knit fabrics together. Some knits have their yarn running along the length of the fabric, others have their yarn running across the width. The columns of stitches that run the length of a knitted fabric are called wales, and the stitches running across form rows. Because of its construction, knitted fabric has some give in every direction, so it is ideal for form-fitting garments, but is less often used for furnishings. Most knits will need to be overstitched to finish the edges and prevent unravelling.

Jersey is a knit fabric – T-shirts are most often produced using a jersey fabric made from a lightweight yarn.

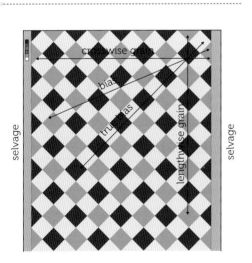

NONWOVEN FABRICS

This category includes fabrics such as felt, interfacing, lace and net. Interfacing is a compressed synthetic fabric used as a backing to the main project fabric, particularly in dressmaking and tailoring, to give extra body, shaping and support. Lace and net are made of yarns that are knotted into intricate patterns, and can either be machine- or handmade.

Note

The fabric thickness and weight will affect needle choice, tension and stitch length. Your sewing machine manual should provide guidance. Buy thread at the same time that you buy your fabric. Since thread appears darker on the spool, lay a strand on the fabric to check you have the right colour to match.

FABRIC COMPOSITION

Fabrics can be made from natural fibres, such as cotton, wool, linen and silk, or synthetic fibres, including polyester, nylon, acrylic and rayon, while others can be made from a blend of natural fibres or from natural and synthetic fibres mixed together in various percentages, such as polycotton, which is a mix of polyester and cotton.

SEWING ON DIFFERENT FABRICS

Pure cotton is the ideal sewing material: it feels good to handle, drapes well, and washes and presses easily. There's a wide range of colours, patterns, weaves and textures. Many modern synthetics or natural/synthetic mixes are very easy to work too. Yet one of the joys of sewing is the chance to use different fabrics, so follow these tips.

SILK

The most beautiful items can be made of silk – the play of light and shade can bring a whole new dimension to the design. Silk is available in many weights and textures and in every colour of the rainbow. It is easy to press and pleasing to work, but it is very slippery and frays easily. Use very fine pins and keep all pinning within the seam allowance as silk will retain pin marks. Cut silk on top of a cotton sheet to stop it sliding around too much, and use very sharp scissors. Hand tack all but the simplest seams. Sheer silks will need a narrow French seam; otherwise use a seam with as little bulk as possible.

VELVET, VELVETEEN AND CORDUROY

Fabrics such as these have a pile or nap – the short fibres have been brushed in one direction, or have raised threads or loops on the surface that are created in the weaving process. Depending on how the light falls on these fabrics, or in which direction they are smoothed, they will look lighter or darker. The nap or pile should run in the same direction on each part, or it will look as if it has been made with two different fabric colours. Use fine pins to avoid marking the pile. When cutting, keep the fabric pile-side up and if you need to place a pattern edge on a fold, fold the fabric with the pile on the outside. When stitching, stitch with the direction of the pile and use a plain seam pressed open. Finish the edges of the seam because these fabrics tend to fray badly (see p. 122 for some options).

LEATHER AND SUEDE

Some areas of animal skin will be thinner than others, so when planning out a project avoid letting these fall where they will be subject to strain.

Place all pattern pieces in the same direction and use pins only within the seam allowance.

Do all fitting and pattern checking in a fabric toile first because once the leather or suede has been stitched the holes made by the needle are permanent. Use a wedge-pointed leather needle – its tip will pierce the surface cleanly. When stitching round corners, make the corner blunt rather than very pointed. When seams are finished, stick the seam allowances down with a liquid adhesive suitable for leather. For an invisible finish at the hem you can turn the edge under and stick it in place with no stitching at all.

STRETCH FABRIC

Use very fine pins and place them at right angles to the edge. When cutting, try not to stretch the edge out of shape. It is best to hand tack seams before stitching because this will help to keep the layers aligned as you sew. Snip through a tacking stitch every 10cm (4in) or so; this will allow you to stretch the fabric slightly by holding it both in front and behind the presser foot as you stitch, keeping it under tension to keep the stitching fairly loose, so the thread will not break under strain when the seam stretches in use. When sewing knitted fabrics, use a ballpoint needle, as the rounded tip will tend to slide between the yarn threads rather than piercing them.

CUTTING FABRIC

To keep your fabric-cutting scissors sharp, never use them for anything else. You can use your dining room or kitchen table, or even a clean floor, for cutting fabric, but be careful not to damage the surface. Cut in smooth strokes, not in little jerky movements. Generally fabric is cut on the straight grain of the fabric, but sometimes you will need to cut fabric on the bias, when making bias binding strips, for example (see p. 136). Fabric cut on the bias stretches and must be handled with care.

CUTTING FABRIC ON THE BIAS

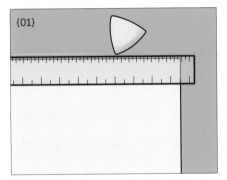

Start by making sure that the fabric is absolutely straight and square to the grain before you begin. To find the straight of grain, align the edge of a piece of paper with the selvage. Place a ruler along the opposite edge and draw a line along it in chalk. This line will be on the straight of grain.

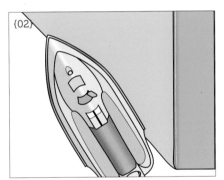

Align the bottom edge of the fabric with the marked straight of grain line and press.

All the fabric pieces for the fancy fabric flowers (p. 10) are cut on the bias.

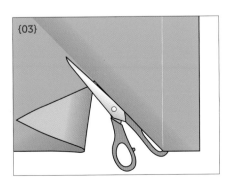

Turn the fabric so you are facing the direction you wish to cut and open the fold. Cut carefully along the pressed crease, making sure that you do not stretch or distort the fabric as you work.

Note

The mixing of fibres is often done to improve the qualities of the original fibre – to make it more hardwearing, easier to wash, less prone to creasing or to create a better drape. It is important to keep a note of the composition of the fabric you are using so that you can care for the finished item properly when it needs cleaning or pressing.

Seams and hems

Sewing two pieces of fabric together to create a stitched seam is a basic construction method for any project, and machine-stitched seams will almost certainly be stronger than hand-stitched ones. As for hems, a simple, turned-up, slipstitched hem is often used, but you can also use your sewing machine for neat, quick-to-stitch hems.

MACHINE SEAMS

Here's everything you need to know to sew a basic straight seam as well as techniques for working a neat curved seam too. In addition you'll need to get to grips with French seams if you want to make the beautiful trapeze sundress on p. 46.

PINNING FOR MACHINE SEWING

Place the pieces of fabric right sides together, aligning the raw edges. Pin the layers together with the pins at right angles to the edge. Position the heads so the pins can be removed efficiently as you stitch: to the right if you are right-handed, or to the left if you are left-handed.

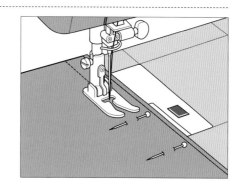

More often than not the seam allowance will be 1cm (3/8in) or 1.5cm (5/8in), but when joining small pieces of fabric, to make the shrews (p. 24) for example, a 6mm (1/4in) seam allowance is more usual.

PLAIN STRAIGHT SEAM

This is the simplest form of seam, designed to hold two or more layers of fabric securely together.

𝒩ote

There is no need to mark the seamline – just follow the guidelines etched on the needle plate. When working with slippery fabrics or stitching more complex seams, it may be safer to tack the pieces together before stitching.

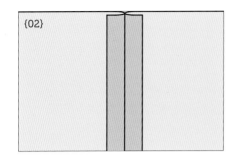

{01}

Pin the pieces of fabric right sides together, aligning the raw edges. Sew the seam on the machine, using a simple straight stitch with a short run of backstitching at each end of the seam to secure.

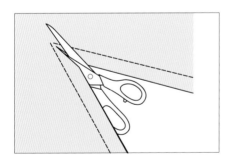

{02}

Remove any tacking threads or remaining pins and press the seam, either with the seam allowances opened out flat – as seen here – or with both pressed to one side.

TRIMMING TO NEATEN SEAMS

Cutting away excess fabric in the seam allowance before you turn corners and points right side out will eliminate bulk and help you to achieve a neat pointed finish. When turning right side out, ease the fabric into a sharp point using the end of a blunt knitting needle or bodkin, but be careful not to push it right through the stitching.

𝒩ote

If you need to grade or clip the seam allowances, do this before you finish the edges (see p. 122).

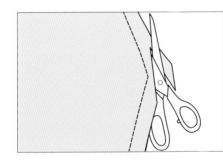

GRADING SEAMS
When working with thicker fabrics or with several layers, seams can become quite bulky and they may not lie flat. To eliminate some of the bulk you can trim the seam allowances down so that each one is a different width.

OBTUSE (WIDE) ANGLE
Clip off the corner within the seam allowance, close to the stitching but being careful not to cut through it.

ACUTE (SHARP) ANGLE
Use a pair of small, sharp scissors to clip into the tip of the point within the seam allowance, being careful not to cut through the stitching.

INTERSECTING SEAMS

In some instances you may need to join two seamed sections. Follow these steps to ensure that the seam in each section aligns perfectly across the join.

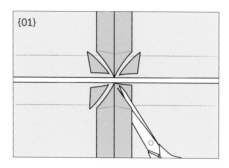

{01}

Press the seams open on each section. To reduce bulk at the intersection on bulkier fabrics, cut the ends of the seam allowances of the original seams into a point on both sections.

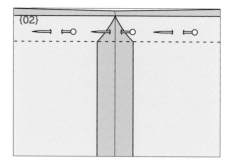

{02}

With the sections right sides together, match the stitched seams exactly, so they will run straight across the new seam at a right angle. Pin or tack along the new seam so the alignment cannot slip as you sew.

Note

As you stitch across the seam allowances at the intersection you will be stitching through four layers. Most machines can handle this easily, but if the fabric is very bulky you may have to turn the hand wheel to ease the needle gently through the layers.

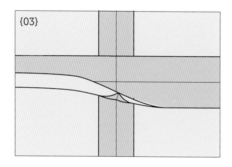

{03}

Press the new seam open flat. On the right side of the fabric, the four seams should form a perfect cross with right-angle lines.

The easy peasy patchwork quilt (p. 30) provides the beginner stitcher with plenty of plain straight seam sewing practice; it is important to align the seams perfectly when sewing the rows of squares together.

CURVED SEAMS

Shaped seams are stitched in the same way as a plain straight seam, but they often need notching or clipping to remove excess fabric so the seam will lie flat.

FOR A CONCAVE (INWARD) CURVE

To create a concave curve on the right side, stitch the seam and then make little clips or snips in the seam allowance just up to – but not through – the line of stitching. The smaller the curve, the closer together the clips need to be, but keep them evenly spaced. When the item is turned right way out the edges of the clips will overlap so the pressed seam will lie flat.

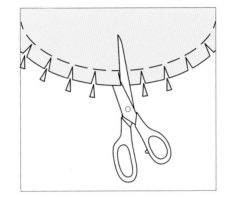

FOR A CONVEX (OUTWARD) CURVE

To create a convex curve on the right side, stitch the seam and then cut wedge-shaped notches from the seam allowance to eliminate excess fullness. The smaller the curve, the closer together the notches need to be – but keep the notches fairly narrow to avoid a jagged look to the seam when the item is turned right way out.

When making the kimono top (p. 14), it is important to snip into the seam allowance under the arm and to clip into the curves around the neck to ensure that the fabric lies smoothly on the finished garment.

SEAM FINISHES

Finishing off the raw edges inside an item will give your projects a more professional look, particularly if the item is not lined and the seams are on show. Protecting the raw edges of the fabric will also minimise possible fraying and so prolong the finished item's life. The finish you choose will depend on the fabric you are using and the type of project being stitched.

PINKED

Stitch a plain seam, then trim both raw edges with pinking shears. The seam can be pressed open or to one side. For extra security, a line of stitching can be added within the seam allowance on each side next to the pinked edge.

Suitable for: Most seams, as long as the fabric is not prone to fraying.

Advantages: Quick and easy to do; doesn't add bulk.

Disadvantages: Not suitable for fabrics that fray; not as neat as other methods; requires special scissors.

DOUBLE-STITCHED

Stitch a plain seam and press to one side. Make a second line of stitching next to the first working within the seam allowance and using either a multi-stitch zigzag or straight stitching (see below). Trim your seam allowance close to the second line of stitching.

Suitable for: Any seam subject to strain; sheer fabrics and lace.

Advantages: Easy to do.

Disadvantages: Seam allowance cannot be pressed open.

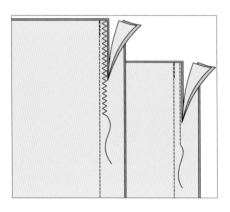

ZIGZAG STITCHED

Stitch a plain seam and press open. Zigzag stitch along each raw edge. If the seam is to be pressed to one side, you can zigzag both raw edges together.

Suitable for: Most seams, but particularly light- to medium-weight fabrics that may fray.

Advantages: Effective at preventing fraying; adds little bulk.

Disadvantages: May not look as neat as other methods.

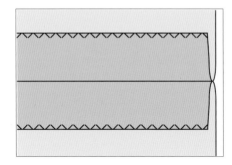

TURNED AND ZIGZAGGED

Stitch a plain seam and press open. Turn under a very narrow hem along each raw edge and zigzag close to the fold.

Suitable for: Lightweight fabrics or fabrics that tend to fray.

Advantages: Looks neater than a plain zigzag stitched edge; will prevent fraying.

Disadvantages: Takes extra time; adds some bulk.

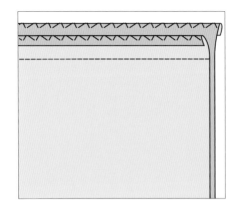

FRENCH SEAM

This is perfect for working straight seams on sheer fabrics. It is an enclosed seam which means that the edges are enclosed during the process of making the seam, so no raw edge finishing is required. The trimming and seam allowance advice given will vary depending on the pattern you are using, so be sure to follow the instructions carefully for working the side seams on the sundress on p. 50.

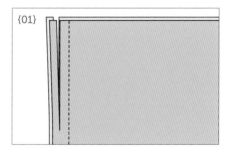

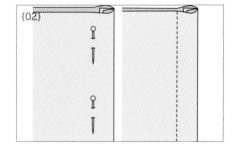

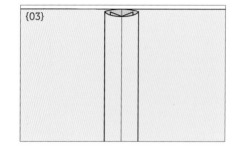

With wrong sides together, stitch the seam 1cm (³⁄₈in) from the edge. Trim the seam allowance to a scant 3mm (¹⁄₈in) and press open.

Fold the fabric right sides together along the stitching line. Pin and stitch a second seam on the seamline.

Check on the right side that no threads from the raw edges are protruding – clip off carefully. Press flat or to one side as advised.

Note

As you develop your stitching skills and expand the range of fabrics you stitch with, you'll need to research other options, such as, for example, the flat-fell seam for working with heavy-duty denim.

French seams encase raw edges within the seam itself, which is ideal when working with viscose for the trapeze sundress (p. 46).

HEMS

A hem can be hand or machine stitched – the choice will depend on both the weight of the fabric to be hemmed and whether the hemming is to be unnoticeable or used as a decorative feature.

MARKING A HEMLINE

When measuring a hem on a garment, try to wear similar height shoes to those that will be worn with it. Ask someone to help by measuring up from the floor and marking the hemline with pins as a first step. Although pinning is often sufficient to hold a hem until it is stitched, tacking it in place will ensure accuracy and a straight line. Once tacked, try the garment on again to check the length before final stitching.

Note

The hem is usually the last thing to be stitched, but it is worth taking time to get it right and that starts with the marking of the hemline. An uneven or badly stitched hem will be hard to miss.

SINGLE HEM

With a single-fold hem, just one layer of fabric is pressed to the wrong side and the raw edge will require neatening. Single hems are ideal for fabrics that do not fray, and also for heavier fabrics where a double-fold hem would be too obvious or bulky.

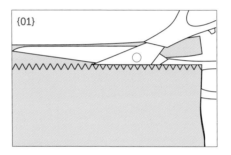

Measure the hem, then fold and press the bottom of the hem to mark it. Open the fold out flat and set the sewing machine to a zigzag stitch. Sew a line of stitching through the single layer of the hem allowance, working 2.5cm (1in) below the foldline. Trim the raw edge close to the line of zigzag stitching, being careful not to cut through the stitching thread.

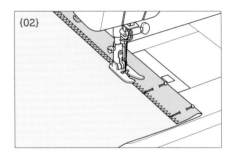

Fold the hem up along the original foldline and pin in place. For an invisible hem, secure the hem in position with hemming stitch (see p. 99), or sew a line of straight machine stitching just below the zigzag stitching.

DOUBLE HAND-STITCHED HEM

With a double hem, the edge is folded twice, so the raw edge is enclosed and there is no need to neaten it. A double hem is also a good way to incorporate extra fabric in the hem to allow for the item to be lengthened later.

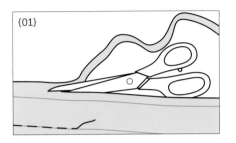

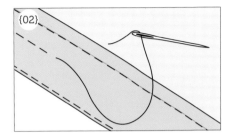

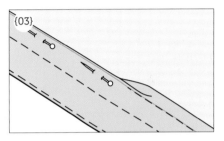

Measure the hem, then fold and press along the hemline to mark it. Fold over the raw edge and press again. Tack along the foldlines to mark them and trim the raw edge to 6mm (¼in) from the second fold.

Fold up the hem along the hemline, aligning the seams as far as possible – you may need to ease in places if the garment is very flared. Tack all the way around the hem through the centre of the fold.

Turn under the raw edge along the second marked line and pin in place, adjusting any easing so all seams are aligned. Hem along the fold, using hemming stitch or slipstitch (see p. 99). Remove pins as you work and any tacking when you have finished.

MACHINE-STITCHED HEM

A machine-stitched hem is generally narrower than a hand-stitched one and the stitching will inevitably show on the right side. If the item is very flared, follow the instructions for a machine-stitched circular hem (see p. 127).

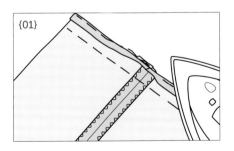

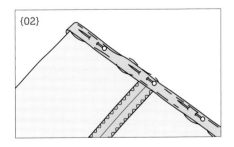

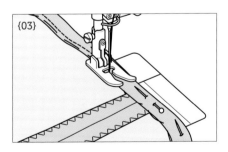

Measure, mark and tack two foldlines, one 6mm (¼in) from the raw edge and the other 1cm (⅜in) in from the first. Turn the first fold under; press.

Turn under the second fold and press. Pin or tack the double layer of fabric in position all round, aligning any seams as you work.

Working on the wrong side, edgestitch close to the inner foldline, removing any pins as you work. Remove any tacking and press.

MACHINE-STITCHED BLIND HEM

Using a blind hem presser foot, it is possible to stitch a hem that will be almost invisible on the right side and quicker to work than a double hand-stitched hem.

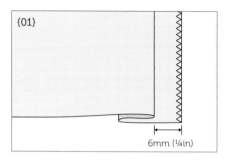

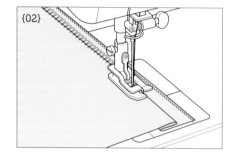

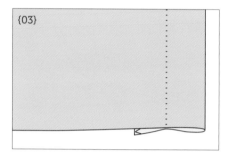

Mark the hem and zigzag along the raw edge. Fold along the hemline, and then fold the fabric back again so the second fold is 6mm (¼in) from the zigzag edge.

Select a wide zigzag stitch and slide the fabric under the blind hem presser foot, positioning it so that the needle will just pierce the edge of the fold when in the left-hand position. Stitch, keeping the folded edge aligned with the guide on the foot.

When you have finished stitching, fold the hem back and press in place. The tip of each zigzag stitch catches the fabric on the right side so the hem is both strong and almost invisible.

TOPSTITCHED HEM

The topstitching gives a crisp finish to the hem and can be worked in a contrast thread for a decorative effect. Topstitching thread tends to be thicker than normal because the stitches are supposed to be visible as part of the design.

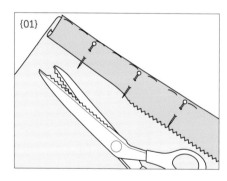

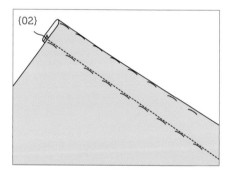

Measure and mark the hem by pressing it and then tack along the foldline. Turn the hem under along the foldline, trim along the raw edge with pinking shears, and then turn the raw edge under. Pin the hem in place, matching seams. Tack the hem in place and remove pins.

From the right side, topstitch around the hem to hold all layers in place. Use the guidelines marked on the needle plate of the sewing machine to keep the stitching line the same distance from the folded edge all the way around. Remove any tacking and press.

MACHINE-STITCHED CIRCULAR HEM

This quick and easy machine method will give a perfectly even narrow hem on a completely circular item. It is a great technique to use if you don't have the special rolled hem foot for your machine.

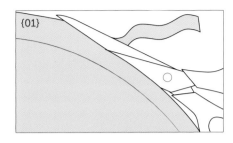

{01}

Measure and mark the hemline. Trim the raw edge so it is an equal distance from the marked hemline all around, making sure you leave at least 6mm (¼in) width of fabric.

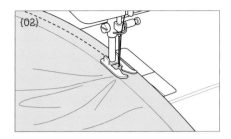

{02}

Working on the right side of the fabric, machine stitch a line of straight stitching exactly 3mm (⅛in) away from the marked hemline all around the hem, between the hemline and the raw edge.

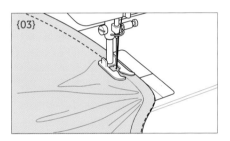

{03}

Turn under the hem to the wrong side along the stitched line and press into place. Working on the right side, sew a second line of machine stitching all around the marked hemline.

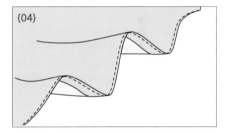

{04}

Turn under the hem to the wrong side along the second stitched line and press into place. Pull gently on the seam all around to ease any puckers. Working on the right side, topstitch close to the edge all around the hem.

Note

To hand stitch a curved seam, measure and mark the hemline. Pink or zigzag stitch the raw edge and tack the foldline. Run a line of gathering stitches 6mm (¼in) in from the zigzagging. Turn up the hem along the tacked foldline and tack the hem in place about 6mm (¼in) from the fold. Matching the seams, pin the hem in place (placing the pins vertically), pulling up the gathering thread as you work to spread the fabric evenly and ease in fullness. Use a blind herringbone stitch to sew the hem in place, removing pins as you work (this is worked like the hemming stitch [p. 99] but the diagonal stitches are longer and overlap). Remove all tacking once finished.

ROLLED HEM

This hem is ideal for circular items or for hemming very fine fabrics such as silk, because it creates a very narrow unobtrusive hem. It requires a special rolled hem presser foot (see p. 109).

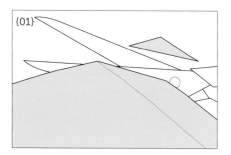

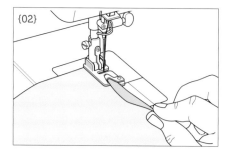

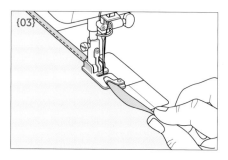

On the raw edge to be hemmed, fold over about 3mm (⅛in) for the first 6.5cm (2½in) and press lightly. To start the hem off neatly, it helps to trim a triangle from the corner 4.5mm (³/₁₆in) wide and 6mm (¼in) long.

With the edge of the fabric folded over, place it under the presser foot. Gently pull the raw edge into the curl of the foot. Begin stitching slowly, ensuring that the fabric is making a complete loop in the curl. Gently lift and guide the fabric slightly towards the left side of the foot to keep the fabric feeding smoothly and evenly.

Sew slowly to check how the fabric is reacting to being rolled, and establish exactly how to hold the fabric so that it feeds smoothly. Each fabric is different, so test-hem a piece before sewing your project.

If your machine has a rolled hem presser foot, it would be ideal for sewing the hem on the trapeze sundress (p. 46).

MITRED HEM

A mitred hem is used for the corners on many home furnishing items, such as tablecloths and place mats, but this technique can also be adapted to give a neat finish when a horizontal hem meets a vertical facing, such as on jacket fronts and skirt slits.

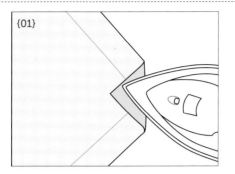

{01}

At the corner, turn up the hem allowance and press along the hemline in both directions. Open the hem out flat again and turn up the corner into a triangle, aligning the pressed lines. Press across the base of the triangle to make a diagonal crease.

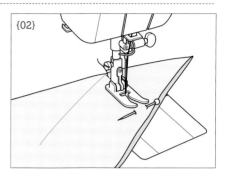

{02}

Open the corner triangle flat again and then fold the item through the corner diagonally with right sides together so the raw edges and the folded hemlines align. Pin in place, then stitch along the diagonal crease made in step 1.

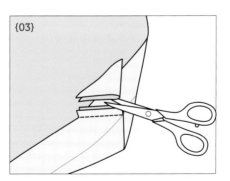

{03}

Trim off the excess fabric from the corner and press the seam open. Repeat on all corners. Turn the corners right side out, to the wrong side of the fabric. Turn under the raw edges on each side of the hem and pin in place. Stitch the hem.

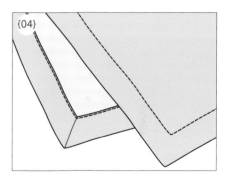

{04}

The finished corners should have neat mitres on one side and a plain corner on the other.

Zips and buttons

A closure can be purely functional or decorative too, and there is a wide choice of different options for you to add or to make using your sewing machine. Even the most basic machine can stitch a buttonhole or zip.

ZIPS

The most common closure used is the zip. Many people feel daunted by the very thought of inserting a zip, but there really is no need.

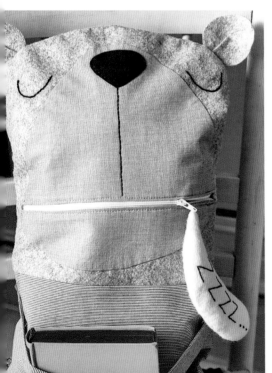

BUYING ZIPS

Zips can have plastic, nylon or metal teeth, which are mounted on a coloured tape. Closed-end zips have a bottom stop at one end and are used for skirts, trousers, dresses and home décor projects. Separating (open-ended) zips are used for the front opening of cardigans and jackets.

Zips come in two basic types: conventional and concealed. Conventional zips have exposed teeth; concealed zips have coils that roll inward and are hidden by the zip tape. Zips come in a range of different lengths, weights and colours. Match the weight of the zip to the weight of the fabric you are using.

A conventional zip closure creates the mouth of the dapper bear pyjama case (p. 64).

Conventional zip.

Separating zip.

Concealed zip.

INSERTING A BASIC ZIP

This is the zip technique most often used for making cushions and a variation of this technique has been used to make the fruity floor cushions (p. 72). The zip is usually inserted before the item is assembled, as it is easier to work on flat fabric.

Note

Another zip insertion technique you may encounter is the lapped zip, set so a piece of fabric on one side of the opening covers and conceals the zip teeth. It may be used as a side zip in trousers or a skirt, or at centre back of a dress or blouse.

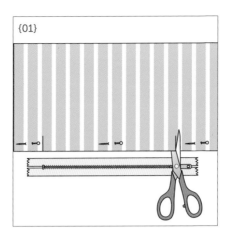

{01}

Line the zip up in position against the raw edge and clip the seam allowances of both layers to mark the two ends. With right sides together, and aligning the cuts, pin the pieces together and stitch from each cut to the edge, backstitching at the cut end to secure.

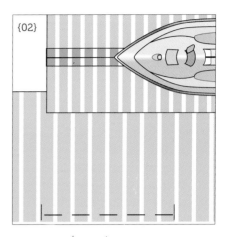

{02}

Machine tack the opening between the two cuts closed. Slitting through one of the stitches every inch or so will make the tacking easier to remove later. Press the seam open.

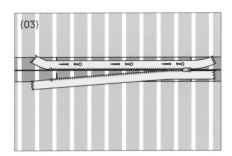

{03}

Lay the fabric flat, right side facing down. Open the zip and pin it in place right side facing down as shown with the teeth very close to the seamline and edges level with the cuts.

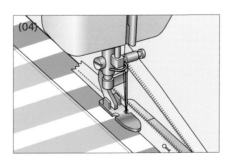

{04}

Using the zipper foot on the machine and keeping the needle on the left, stitch close to the teeth, backstitching at each end. Turn and repeat steps 3 and 4 to stitch the other side.

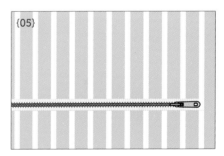

{05}

Remove the tacking, turn the fabric to the right side, and press gently, being careful not to iron over the zip itself. Continue making up the rest of the item in the normal way.

BUTTONS AND BUTTONHOLES

Buttonholes are often an area of concern for beginner stitchers, but practice will give you confidence. Most sewing machines have an automatic four-step buttonhole function, with pre-set stitch settings accessed at the turn of a button, and more expensive machines may have a one-step automatic buttonhole function (see p. 109). If your machine doesn't have either, follow the machine-sewn buttonhole instructions here.

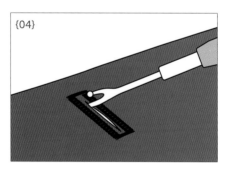

MACHINE-SEWN BUTTONHOLE

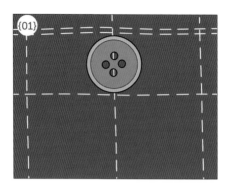

Mark the centre position and length of the buttonhole by tacking guidelines on the right side of the fabric, using the button as a guide: don't sew your buttonholes too close to the edge of the fabric and make them a little larger than the diameter of your chosen button (+3mm/⅛in).

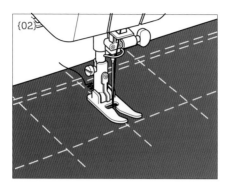

Run a line of straight stitching on each side of the line of the buttonhole opening to stabilise the edge. Set the machine to zigzag stitch, with a short length and width setting, and stitch a row of zigzag stitching along one long side of the buttonhole.

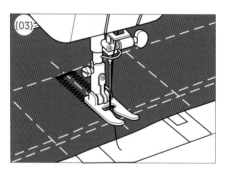

With the needle down, raise the foot and turn the garment 180-degrees; adjust the stitch width to make a few long stitches across the full buttonhole width to reinforce the end. Work the second side and end in the same way.

Set the stitch width at 0 to make a few stitches to secure the thread end. Pull the thread ends through to the back and trim close. Use a seam ripper to slit the buttonhole open on the centre line.

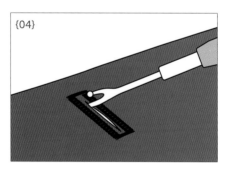

Perfect your buttonhole stitching skills by making the skirt on p. 84.

SEWING ON A BUTTON

Some buttons have a loop or shank on the back, which you sew through to attach the button. It also holds the button above the surface of the fabric to allow for the thickness of the upper fabric layer. Other buttons must be stitched through the holes provided (two-hole and four-hole) and may require a thread shank.

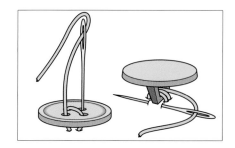

TO MAKE A THREAD SHANK

Place a matchstick or toothpick on top of the button and sew over it. Remove the stick, lift the button, and wind the thread around the extra length of thread between the button and the garment. Bring the needle to the underside of the garment and fasten with several small stitches.

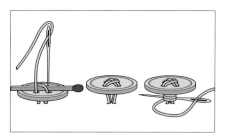

SELF-COVERING BUTTONS

If you can't find exactly the right buttons for your project, you can make your own from scraps of your favourite fabrics using a self-covering button kit. (Note: If the button kit has instructions that differ from those below, follow them instead.)

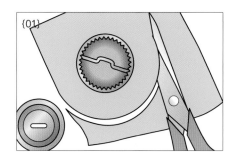

{01}

Using the button or the template provided in the kit, cut a circle of fabric around 1.5cm (⅝in) wider than the top of the button.

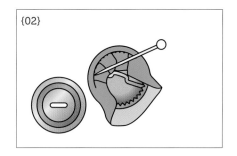

{02}

Place the button top in the centre of the wrong side of the fabric. Use a pin to push the excess fabric so that it catches on the teeth around the edge of the button top. Make sure all the fabric is securely held in place.

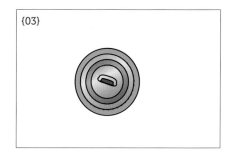

{03}

Line up the back of the button on the reverse of the button top and press it firmly into place until it snaps into position.

Trimming and binding

For most projects the raw edges will need to be finished off in some way, but you may not want to make a simple hem. If you are looking for something more decorative, you can use your sewing machine to add a binding or trim quite quickly and easily, and the basic how-tos are described here.

TRIMMING

The addition of a trim to a homemade project or to a store-bought item is a wonderful way to personalise them. There are many different trims available, such as ricrac, braid, lace or ribbon, in a variety of colours and widths. Trims can be added to an edge or inserted in a seam.

ATTACHING FRINGE TRIMS

Fringed trims have a tape header at the top, which can be used to attach them. Normally, the fringe is applied to the item by stitching through the header, but it can also be inserted in a seam (see Attaching In-seam Trims, opposite).

Pin the fringe in place, then machine or hand stitch with matching thread. If the fringe has a wide heading, stitch along both the top and bottom edges.

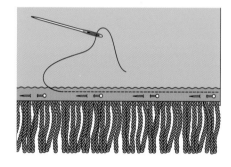

If the tape header is fairly plain, you can stitch it on with zigzag stitch or one of the decorative machine stitches.

Note

Trims cover or decorate an edge and binding is a method of enclosing the edge in a narrow strip of fabric.

A tassel trim adds a touch of chic to the kimono top (p. 14).

ATTACHING IN-SEAM TRIMS

When inserting a trim in a seam, it must be placed between the two layers of fabric before they are stitched.

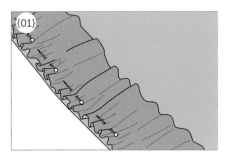

Lay the trim – in this case a double frill – on the front piece of fabric, right sides together. Note that the frill is pointing towards the centre, so when the item is turned right side out again it will be on the outside.

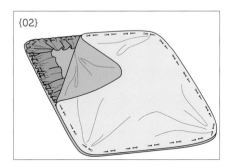

Lay the back piece of fabric right side down on top and align the raw edges. Stitch in place, turn the item right side out and press.

GATHERS

Gathering fabric is a simple technique that can be used in many situations: at the waistband of skirts or trousers to reduce fabric width at the waistline; at curtain headings to soften the effect; or to make frills or ruffles to trim garments and accessories.

STRAIGHT STITCH GATHERING

Gathering with machine stitching using a long stitch will give the most even result. Use a strong, good-quality thread.

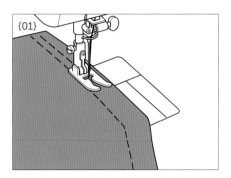

Set the stitch length on the machine at its longest and loosen the upper tension slightly. Stitch a straight line just inside the seamline, then stitch a parallel line around 6mm (¼in) away within the seam allowance.

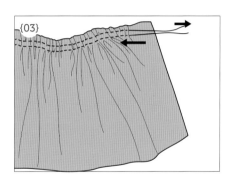

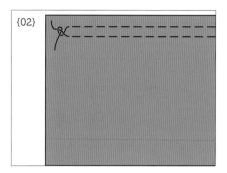

At one end of the stitching, tie the two top threads together on the right side of the fabric and the two bobbin threads together on the wrong side. This will stop the fabric from sliding off the stitching as you begin to gather.

At the untied end, pull both bobbin threads together to gather up the fabric to the required length, easing the fabric along the threads. Fasten off the bobbin threads to secure the end, then adjust the gathers along the length so they are even.

JOINING GATHERED AND FLAT FABRIC

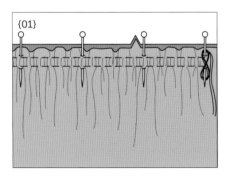

{01}

With right sides together, pin the gathered edge to the flat edge, matching any notches, marks or seams. Check the gathers are even along the length and adjust if necessary. Once correctly adjusted, you can secure the gathering threads in a figure of eight around the final pin.

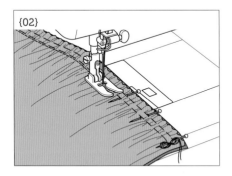

{02}

With the machine at normal stitch setting and tension, place the fabric in the machine with the gathered side uppermost. Stitch along the seamline. Unpick and remove any gathering threads showing on the right side after the seam has been stitched.

BINDING

Binding is a narrow band of fabric that encloses a raw edge and can be made in a matching or contrasting fabric. Binding strips are cut on the straight of grain or on the bias, depending on where they are to be used; if sewn around curved shapes, binding strips must be cut on the bias.

MAKING BIAS BINDING

Bias binding is cut on the true bias of the fabric for maximum stretch, so it is ideal for binding both curved sections and straight edges. Making your own bias binding enables you to match the fabric used in your sewing project exactly and gives you a much greater choice than when purchasing ready-made bias binding. You can cut fabric stips on the bias (see p. 117), but when longer lengths of binding are required the following method is useful.

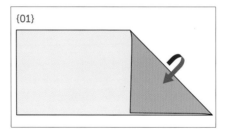

{01}

Fold the crosswise grain of the fabric to the lengthwise grain – the easiest way to do this is to make sure the end of the length is straight on the grain then fold it down to line up with the selvage. The diagonal fold is the true bias. Cut the piece of fabric along the foldline to remove a triangle of fabric.

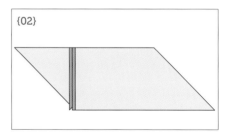

{02}

Stitch the triangle to the other edge of the length of fabric to make a parallelogram. Press the seam open.

Note

A binding can add a decorative emphasis to soft furnishings and home accessories such as placemats, tablecloths and curtain edges.

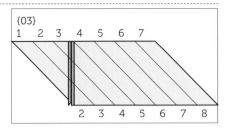

Mark a series of lines parallel with the cut edge set apart by twice the width you want the binding to be. So, if you want 2.5cm (1in) wide binding, space the lines 5cm (2in) apart. Number the bands as 1, 2, 3, etc., along the top edge, using an air-erasable marker. Along the bottom edge, mark band 1 as number 2 and carry on numbering 3, 4, etc, to the end.

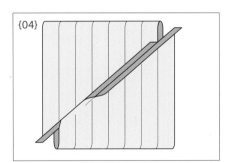

With right sides together, bring the edges round and match the numbers, so 2 lines up with 2, 3 with 3, etc. The first and the last numbers will not match up with anything. Stitch to join the ends with a 1.5cm (⅝in) seam allowance, creating a tube of fabric. Cut along the marked line, which now runs around the tube in a continuous spiral from top to bottom.

JOINING BINDING STRIPS

For very long edges you will almost certainly need to join two strips of binding together to get the length you need. Join the strips of binding before you fold the side edges over.

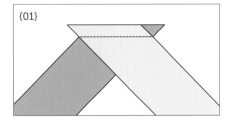

Pin the strips right sides together – they will run at right angles to each other. Stitch together with a 1cm (⅜in) seam allowance.

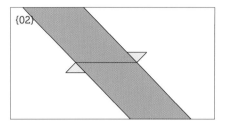

Press the seam open and trim off the protruding points. Fold over one or both edges of the strip as required.

USING A BIAS BINDING MAKER

When you have cut your bias strip you will want to fold over both raw edges to neaten them. If you are making a standard width of binding, a bias binding maker will make this job quick and easy. It is simple to use – just pull the strip through and it turns the edges under ready to press in place. If you are making very wide bias binding, you will have to turn the edges under by hand and press.

A pretty bias binding strip has been used as an alternative to a facing at the waistband of the button-up A-line skirt (p. 84).

BINDING A STRAIGHT EDGE

When you are binding a straight edge, you can use either straight binding or bias binding, the technique is the same whichever you choose.

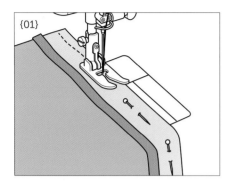

{01}

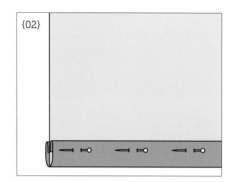

{02}

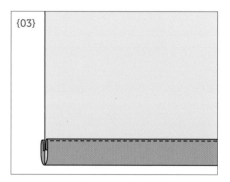

{03}

Open out the fold along one edge of the binding and place it right sides together on the edge to be bound, with raw edges matching. Pin in place. Straight stitch along the foldline of the bias binding nearest the edge, removing the pins as you work. Try to keep the stitching line as straight as possible or your binding will not look neat and straight.

Fold the binding around the raw edge to the wrong side. If you don't want the binding to show on the right side, fold on the stitching line made in step 1. If you want a narrow border, fold on the centre line of the binding as shown.

Stitch close to the folded edge on the wrong side, removing the pins as you work. (If you don't want the stitching to show on the right side, you can slipstitch the binding by hand on the wrong side of the fabric.)

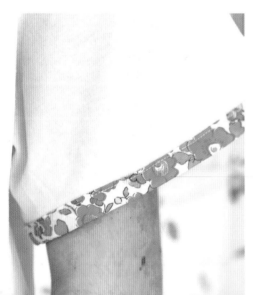

BINDING A CURVED EDGE

When you are binding a curve you will need to use bias binding because the extra stretch allows more leeway for manipulation around the curve. Stretch the bias binding slightly along one edge as you attach it around an outward (convex) curve. Ease the edge slightly to fit an inward (concave) curve.

Bindings are a great way to brighten up a simple garment such as T-shirts (see the heart pocket tee on p. 57).

CONTINUOUS BINDING

For the neatest of finishes, bind the edges of a square or rectangular item with a continuous strip of binding and create a mitre at each corner. Continuous binding can be single (as illustrated in the diagrams) or double – just cut the strip to the appropriate width, which is usually 4cm (1½in) for single-fold and 6.5cm (2½in) for double-fold, although this can vary, so follow the project instructions carefully.

The easy peasy patchwork quilt (p. 30) is made with a continuous double binding, which is ideal for heavily used, frequently laundered items. The strips of fabric here were cut 7.5cm (3in) wide and folded in half before being stitched in place.

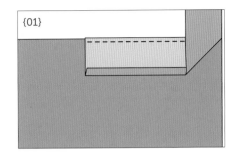

{01}

Beginning in the centre of one side, place the binding strip along one edge of the quilt top, with right sides together and raw edges aligned – the folded edge of the binding should be facing towards the inner part of the quilt. Stitch to within 6mm (¼in) of the edge of the quilt, then backstitch to secure. Remove the quilt from the machine. Fold the binding upwards so a diagonal fold is formed and fingerpress in place.

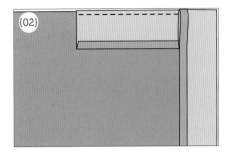

{02}

Now fold the binding strip down to align it with the next edge to be worked, holding the diagonal fold made in step 1 in place with your finger or a pin. Begin stitching down the new edge, starting at the top folded edge of the binding. Repeat at all four corners.

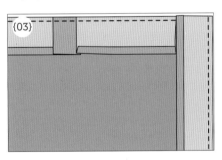

{03}

When you reach your starting position again, fold the last 1cm (⅜in) of the binding over and slide it under the raw edge of the first section of binding.

Note

When you are stitching on binding, be very careful not to stretch it as you sew, particularly if you are using purchased bias binding.

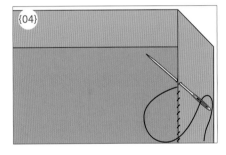

{04}

Turn the binding to the back of the project, and slipstitch the folded edge by hand to the backing fabric as shown in the diagram. When you reach the corner, fold the binding down – a neat mitre will appear (see bottom left of photo) and continue.

PIPING

Piping is a strip of flat, folded fabric inserted into a seam for decoration. Simple piping lies flat and has a soft, rounded look in the seam. Piping that has a cord added inside the fold is known as cording. Corded piping gives a sculptured look.

The shape of the fruity floor cushions (p. 72) – which mimic delicious slices of lime, lemon and orange – is accentuated with corded piping.

SIMPLE PIPING

(01) Make a strip of bias binding twice the width you want the piping to be, plus 3cm (1¼in) for the seam allowances. Fold the strip in half, wrong sides together and with raw edges aligned.

(02) On the seam that is to be piped, place the fabric pieces right sides together with the piping sandwiched in between and all raw edges aligned. Pin or tack together. Stitch along the seamline.

CORDED PIPING

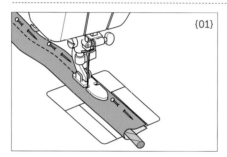
{01}

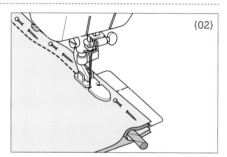
{02}

Make a strip of bias binding three times the width of the cord, plus 3cm (1¼in) for seam allowances. Fold the strip in half, wrong sides together; insert the cord and align the raw edges. Secure with pins or quilter's clips (see p. 74). Stitch as close to the cord as possible, but without catching it (use a piping or zipper foot).

Place the fabric right sides together with the corded piping sandwiched in between and all raw edges aligned. Stitch along the seamline, keeping close to the cord.

JOINING CORDED PIPING

To create a neat join when attaching lengths of corded piping, pull the end out of the fabric casing at each end and trim off the cord ends only so they will exactly meet at the join. Turn under the end of one length of the piping and slide it over the other.

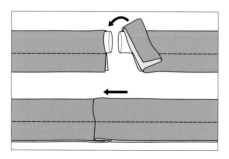

Machine embellishing

Learning stitching techniques can help you to save money by making a whole range of different projects, from clothes to wear to great home accessories. Embellishing techniques, such as machine embroidery and appliqué, are also a good way for you to express your creativity.

FREE-MOTION MACHINE EMBROIDERY

Machine embroidery is quick and fun to do. Even if your machine only has basic straight and zigzag stitches, you can achieve some truly amazing results with free-motion machine embroidery.

Note

Bind the inner or outer ring of the hoop with masking tape or bias binding to help keep fine fabrics taut. Make sure the inner hoop is slightly lower than the outer ring to ensure good, flat contact with the machine. For best results, sharp machine needles are a must.

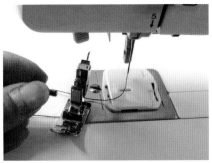

DISENGAGE YOUR FEED DOG

To prepare a standard sewing machine for free-motion machine embroidery, remove the presser foot and lower your feed dog (if available, you can fit and use a darning foot); some machines come with a raised needle plate allowing you to simply cover the feed dog, as shown; either way your machine's manual will tell you what to do. Dropping or covering the feed dog eliminates the machine's grip on the fabric, so you are in control of the movement of the fabric.

SET UP YOUR FABRIC IN A HOOP

To make free-motion embroidery easier, it is necessary to first fit your fabric into an embroidery hoop. Stretch your fabric taut in the outer hoop and push the inner hoop down on top. Make the inner hoop slightly lower than the outer ring to ensure the fabric is really flat on the surface of the machine, then tighten the screw on the side of the hoop.

GET READY TO STITCH

{01}

Set the stitch length at zero and place the hoop in position on the machine, taking care that the needle is in its highest position so that the hoop can be put in without damaging or bending the needle. Lower the foot lever, even though you have removed the foot.

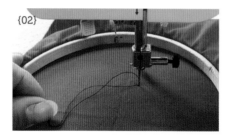

{02}

Put the needle into the fabric using the hand wheel and pull the lower thread to the surface of the fabric to give you two strands of cotton on the hoop. You are now ready to stitch.

(03) Gently hold the two strands of cotton with slack, as this just helps a bit with the first couple of stitches; you can trim these as soon as you get going. Do a few backward and forward stitches to start off with. Start slowly to get the feel of the machine and to see how fast you need to move the fabric.

STITCHING TECHNIQUE

Hold the hoop firmly as you stitch and experiment with your stitching speed, aiming to keep it steady and controlled. You will soon start to get a feel for co-ordinating the stitching and holding the hoop down flat. Practise to gain control of your machine and build confidence. You are aiming for a smooth and steady movement, so try to avoid jerking or moving the hoop too quickly. Do not stitch too close to the hoop as the needle will break if it hits it, and do be particularly careful not to let your fingers stray too near the needle.

Once you have become confident with the basics you can experiment with all sorts of techniques and textures from filling in areas to outlining an appliqué motif.

MACHINE APPLIQUÉ

Appliqué is the technique of applying pieces of fabric or motifs onto a background fabric. It can be used to add extra decorative detail to a small area or to create an entire design, but either way the machine stitching speeds up the process. You can use fusible webbing to attach the appliqué motifs to the background fabric prior to stitching.

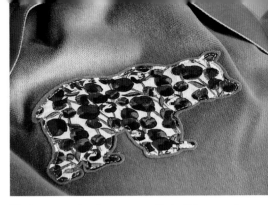

The hot water bottle cover motifs (p. 77) appear to have been satin stitched in place but are actually stitched onto a felt background with straight stitch.

FUSED APPLIQUÉ

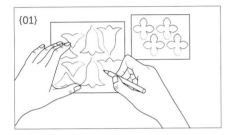

Trace all the appliqué motifs onto the paper backing of pieces of fusible webbing. Aim to use a different piece of fusible webbing for all the appliqué motifs to be cut from each of your chosen fabrics, and lay the shapes close together to save on materials.

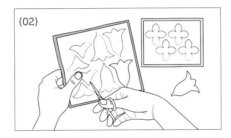

Iron the marked-up pieces of fusible webbing onto the reverse side of the selected fabrics. Cut out each motif leaving the backing paper in place for the moment.

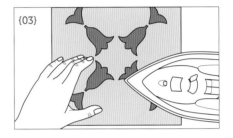

For complicated motifs, mark the centre of the appliqué design on the background fabric with pins, or place the fabric on a light-box with a tracing of the pattern underneath to act as a guide. Peel the backing paper off the appliqué motifs and carefully place the first pieces. Iron into place.

Note

As you are working on the back of the fabric, the motif will be reversed when it is right side up, so do remember to take this into account if your appliqué motif is non-symmetrical or features letters or numbers.

Add the remaining pieces in order and iron to fix in place. Machine stitch around the edges of the appliqué pieces. Set the sewing machine to zigzag stitch with a medium stitch length and a very short stitch width, so that it can be worked very closely like satin stitch; use a darning (embroidery) foot if you have one.

A few tips for making clothes

Learning to sew will give you opportunity to make your own clothes in the fabrics you love. All of the clothing projects in this book use self-drafted patterns, but it is likely you may well be working from a paper pattern for many garments, so we've included a few helpful tips to help you on your way.

PATTERNS

Commercial paper patterns are generally multi-sized and will provide you with a guide to follow and instructions on the order of work.

Note

Take your measurements carefully – ask a friend to help you. Wear form-fitting underwear that is not too tight or constricting, and hold the tape measure comfortably snug but not tight. Record all your measurements on a chart for future reference although sure to check periodically for changes.

TAKING BODY MEASUREMENTS

Taking correct body measurements is key to selecting the pattern size that is right for you, as well as for making self-drafted patterns to fit your body shape exactly. You will need the following set of measurements to cover all options:

Chest circumference: Under the arms with the tape straight across the back.

Bust circumference: Around the fullest part of the bust, keeping the tape level at the back

Hip circumference: Measure around the largest part of your bottom/thighs.

Waist circumference: Measure the natural waistline, which should be the smallest part of the torso. To find it easily when taking other measurements, pin a length of tape or elastic loosely around your waist.

Shoulder length: From neck to shoulder tip. Find your shoulder tip by raising your arm to a horizontal position and feeling for the hollow/pit between the shoulder and arm bones.

Shoulder to bustline: From the shoulder seam to the tip of the bust.

Neck to waistline: Measure from the base of the neck at centre front to the bottom of the tape at the waist.

Shoulder to waistline: Measure from the shoulder seam to the bottom of the tape at the waist.

Overarm to elbow: Measure with the arm slightly bent, from the tip of the shoulder to where the arm bends.

Elbow to wrist: Measure with the arm slightly bent, from where the arm bends to the wrist bone.

Skirt/dress length: Measure from the bottom of waist tape to the desired hem length.

Inside leg: From the crotch to the ankle.

Back length: Put on a thin necklace, or drape a piece of string around your neck. Measure from the place where the necklace falls on the back of your neck to the lower edge of the waist tape.

Bicep: Measure the greatest circumference of your upper arm at the top and just above the elbow.

Underarm: From the armpit to the wrist bone.

Wrist circumference: Around the wrist over the wrist bone.

Crotch depth: Measure from the top of the waist tape at the front, through the legs to the top of the tape at the back.

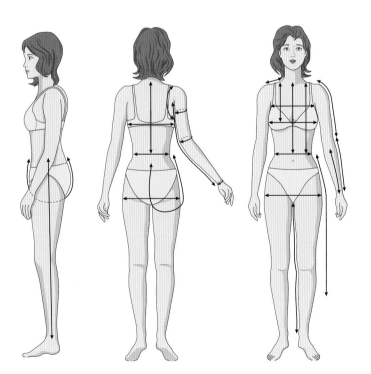

PATTERN SYMBOLS

Pattern pieces contain written directions and symbols such as dots and arrows, an easy to learn shorthand that speeds up your sewing because it shows you which edges to match and where to position details. Here are examples of some common symbols you will encounter in your dressmaking adventures:

 Grainline: Place on straight grain of fabric parallel to the selvage.

 Foldline: Place on fold of fabric.

 Centre line: Centre marking of front or back of garment.

 **Notches and dots:** Location marks for matching key points across different pattern pieces.

 Cutting line: Indicates where to cut and is usually a heavy solid line. There may be several types of lines if the pattern is multi-size.

 Adjustment line: Double lines indicating where you can lengthen or shorten sections of a garment.

 Dart line: Triangular or diamond-shaped lines indicating edges to be joined to shape the garment.

PINNING THE PATTERN

Before you start, identify which pieces of the pattern you will need – most commercial patterns have alternative options, so you may not need every piece supplied for the garment you are making.

Note

With a printed fabric the printing may not be exactly on the straight of grain. If it is only slightly off, it will be better to use the design as your reference for establishing a straight line for pattern placement. If the printing is very off the straight of grain, reject the fabric.

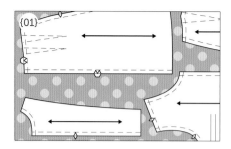

Cut out the required pattern pieces. If the pattern paper is very creased, press gently with a cool iron. Lay pieces roughly in place on the fabric, following the cutting guide layout that comes with the pattern.

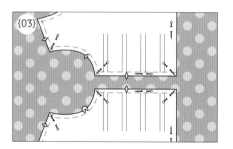

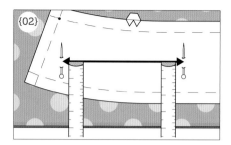

Most pieces will need to be aligned with the straight grain of the fabric and will be marked with a straight-of-grainline – usually a heavy line with an arrowhead at each end. Measure the distance from this line to the nearest selvage at each end and pin the grainline in place first.

For maximum stability, pin all around the edges of the pattern, positioning the pins diagonally into the corners. Pin all the pieces to the fabric before beginning to cut any of them out – you may need to adjust positions slightly to fit them all on.

COPYING PATTERN MARKINGS

Copy the important markings from the pattern to the fabric as soon as you finish cutting the piece out. These include any dots marking construction essentials such as darts or pleats, centre lines, positional marks for adding pockets or buttons, waistline and hemline, and notches. Tailor's tacks are a way of hand stitching placement points on garments for buttonholes, darts, pockets, etc. Alternatively, use one of the marking tools described on p. 93.

SEWING TAILOR'S TACKS

Make a double stitch through the pattern and all layers of the fabric, leaving a loose loop of thread. Snip the loop and remove the pattern. Carefully separate the layers of fabric a little and snip through the threads between the two layers, leaving a few in each piece to mark the point.

Note

There is usually no need to mark seam allowances as you can use the guidelines on the needle plate of your sewing machine as a guide (see p. 106).

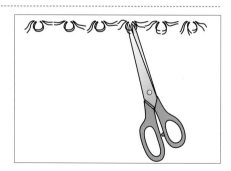

SEWING DARTS

Darts are used to add fullness to allow for the curves of the body at bust, waist, hips and shoulders. They are usually stitched first into flat pieces of fabric before these are joined together into a garment.

SINGLE DART

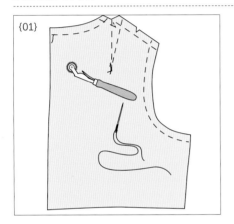

{01}

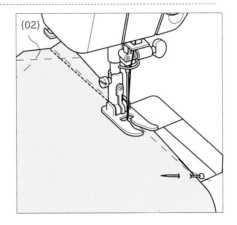

{02}

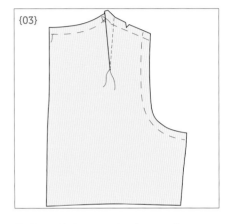

{03}

A single dart will come in from a seamline, usually at the shoulder or side, and the widest point of the dart will be at the seam. Mark the dart line with tailor's tacks. Mark a curved stitching line with tacking.

Fold the fabric in half, right sides together, along the dart's centre line. Sew from the seamline to the point, and a few stitches beyond. Do not backstitch.

Finish with long ends, tie together and snip short. As a general rule, press vertical darts towards the centre of the garment and horizontal darts downwards.

Note

A double-pointed dart combines two darts into one, resulting in a long dart with the widest part occurring at the waist. It tapers to nothing near the bust (or shoulder blade) and near the hip. Pin and stitch as for a single dart, working from the middle to one end, then overlapping several stitches, from the middle to the other end. Clip at its widest point so that it will lie flat.

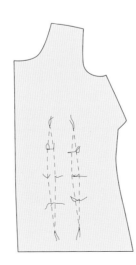

The shaping of the A-line skirt (p. 84) is created by single darts worked at the waistline.

TEMPLATES

Use actual size unless otherwise specified.
Visit www.pavilionbooks.com/howtosew
for full-size templates ready to download.

CAT

HORSESHOE

CAKE

TURTLE

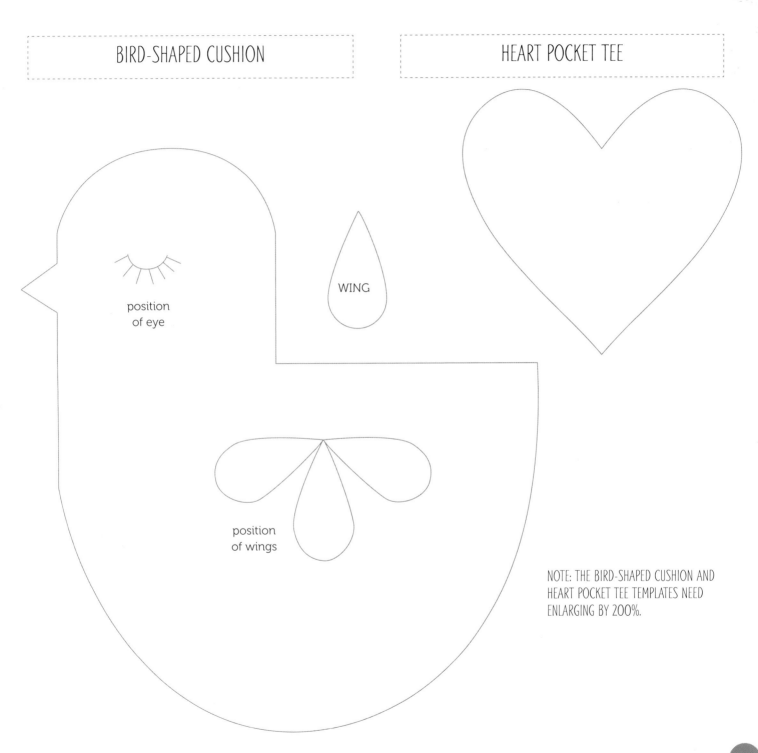

BIRD-SHAPED CUSHION

HEART POCKET TEE

position
of eye

WING

position
of wings

NOTE: THE BIRD-SHAPED CUSHION AND
HEART POCKET TEE TEMPLATES NEED
ENLARGING BY 200%.

FANCY FABRIC FLOWERS

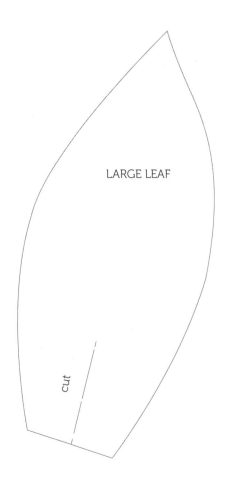

LARGE LEAF

cut

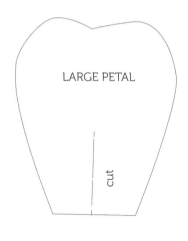

LARGE PETAL

cut

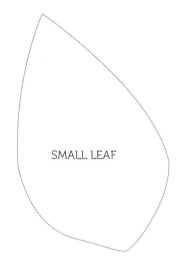

SMALL LEAF

SMALL PETAL

cut

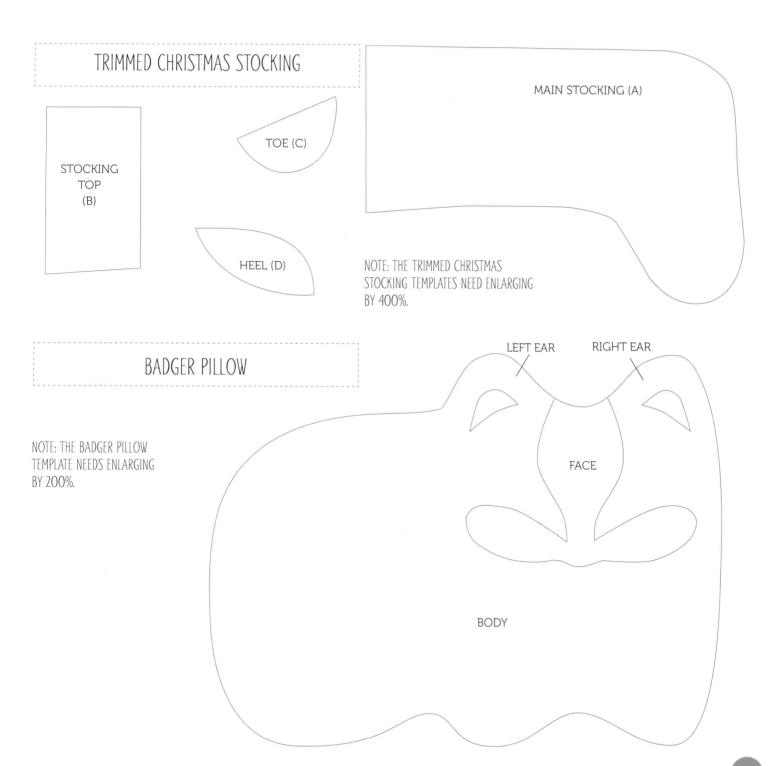

TRIMMED CHRISTMAS STOCKING

STOCKING TOP (B)

TOE (C)

HEEL (D)

MAIN STOCKING (A)

NOTE: THE TRIMMED CHRISTMAS STOCKING TEMPLATES NEED ENLARGING BY 400%.

BADGER PILLOW

NOTE: THE BADGER PILLOW TEMPLATE NEEDS ENLARGING BY 200%.

LEFT EAR

RIGHT EAR

FACE

BODY

FOXY SLEEP MASK

NOTE: THE FOXY SLEEP MASK TEMPLATES NEED
ENLARGING BY 200%.

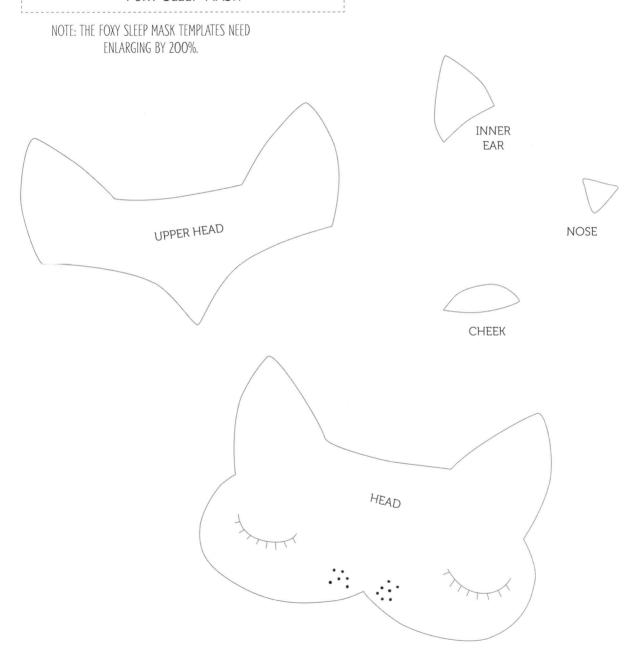

UPPER HEAD

INNER
EAR

NOSE

CHEEK

HEAD

Mollie MAKES HOW TO SEW

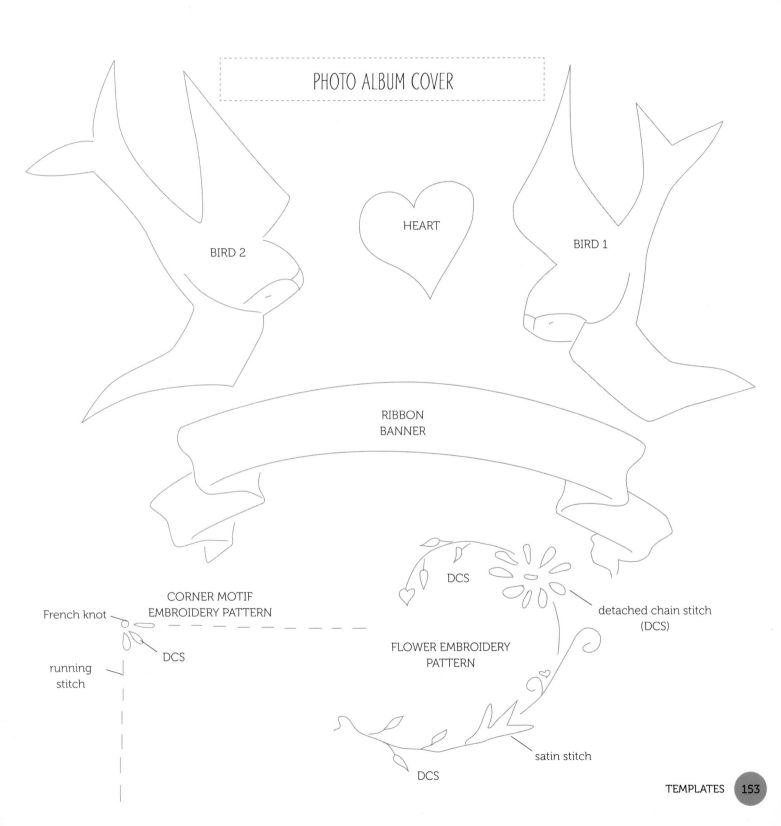

PHOTO ALBUM COVER

BIRD 2

HEART

BIRD 1

RIBBON
BANNER

CORNER MOTIF
EMBROIDERY PATTERN

French knot

DCS

running
stitch

DCS

detached chain stitch
(DCS)

FLOWER EMBROIDERY
PATTERN

satin stitch

DCS

SHREWS IN A SHOE

NOTE: THE SHREWS IN A SHOE TEMPLATES NEED ENLARGING BY 200%.

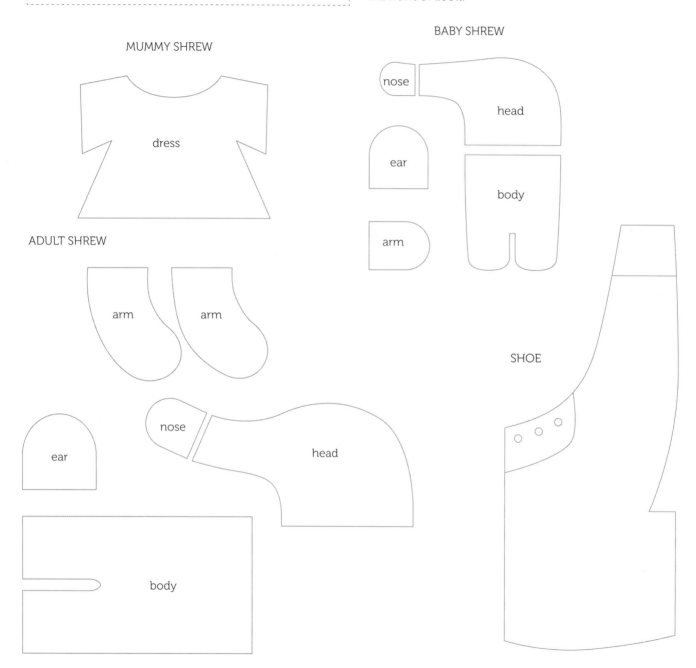

MUMMY SHREW

dress

BABY SHREW

nose

head

ear

body

arm

ADULT SHREW

arm

arm

ear

nose

head

body

SHOE

Mollie MAKES HOW TO SEW

BIRD APPLIQUÉ PEG BAG

NOTE: THE BIRD APPLIQUÉ PEG BAG TEMPLATE
NEEDS ENLARGING BY 200%.

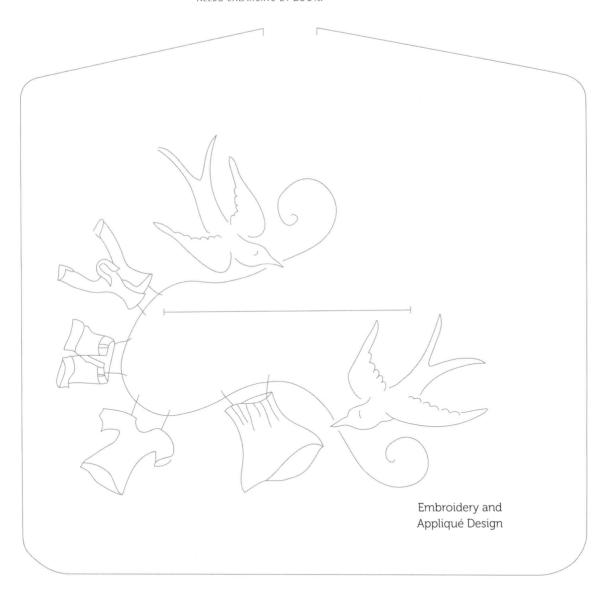

Embroidery and
Appliqué Design

DAPPER BEAR PYJAMA CASE

NOTE: THE DAPPER BEAR PYJAMA CASE TEMPLATES NEED ENLARGING BY 400%.

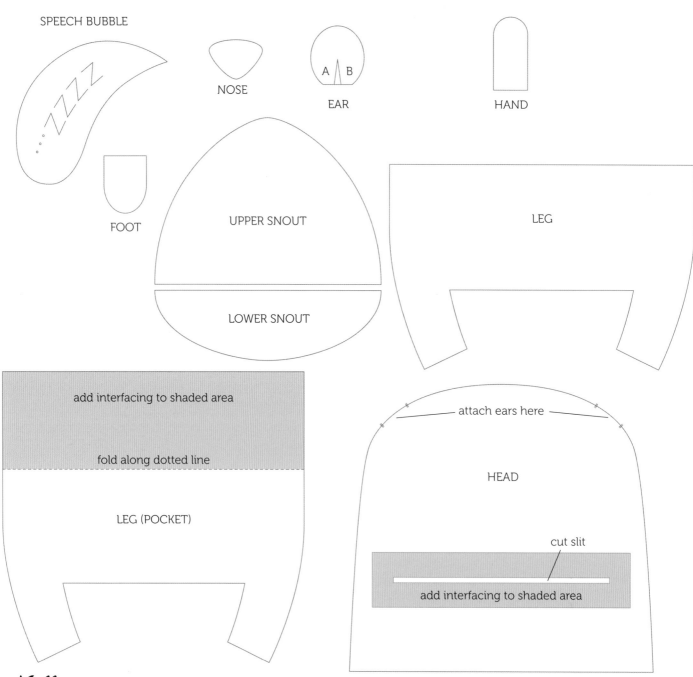

SPEECH BUBBLE

NOSE

EAR

A | B

HAND

FOOT

UPPER SNOUT

LOWER SNOUT

LEG

add interfacing to shaded area

fold along dotted line

LEG (POCKET)

attach ears here

HEAD

cut slit

add interfacing to shaded area

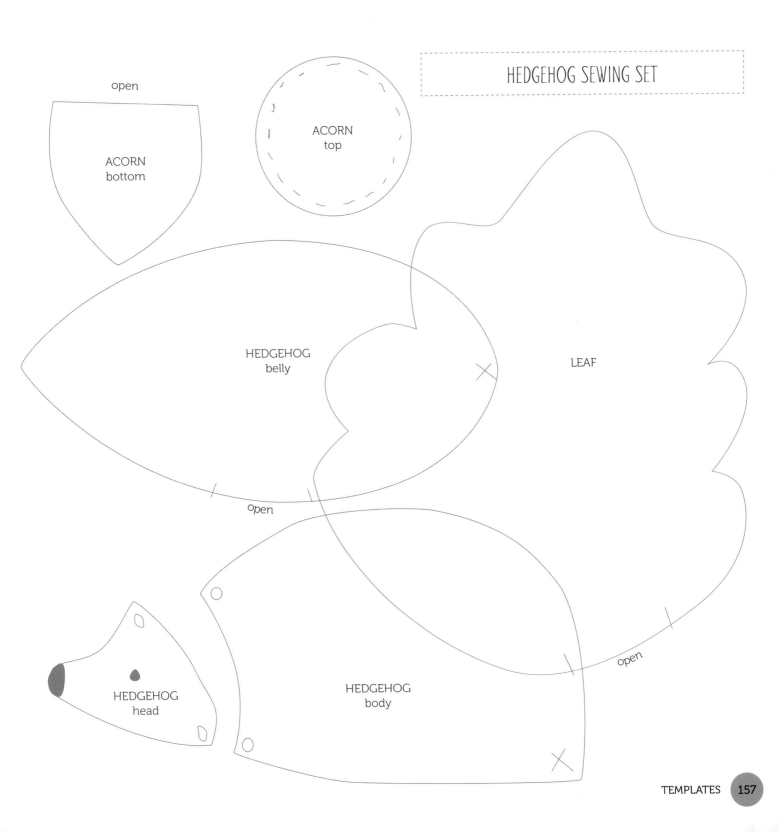

open

ACORN
bottom

ACORN
top

HEDGEHOG SEWING SET

LEAF

HEDGEHOG
belly

open

HEDGEHOG
head

HEDGEHOG
body

open

TRUE LOVE CUSHIONS

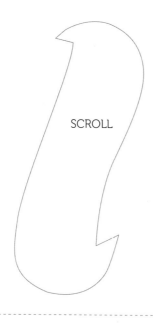

SCROLL

SCROLL END

HEART

NOTE: THE TRUE LOVE CUSHIONS AND
HOT WATER BOTTLE COVERS TEMPLATES
NEED ENLARGING BY 200%.

HOT WATER BOTTLE COVERS

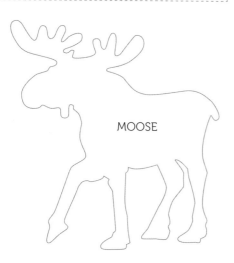

MOOSE

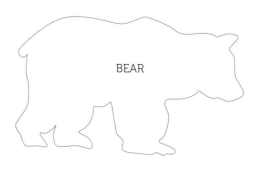

BEAR

INDEX

appliqué 8, 21–3, 34–7
  fused 21–2, 77–8, 80–3, 143
  machine 72, 75, 143

backstitch 6–8, 18–20, 24, 28, 64, 67–70, 80, 83, 98, 112
bias 10, 12, 114, 117
binding 136–9
  bias 46, 48–51, 53–4, 57, 72, 74, 88, 136–7
  continuous 30, 33
  curved edges 53, 57, 138
  joining 30, 33, 53, 57, 72, 74, 137
blanket stitch 6, 9, 103
buttonhole stitch 103
buttonholes 84, 89, 132
buttons
  self-covering 61–2, 133
  sewing on 21–2, 84, 89, 133

Carlill, Emily 82, 83
chain stitch 102
Christmas stocking, trimmed 61–3, 151
Claridge, Sammy 72, 73, 84
Cookson, Theresia 42, 44
corners 112
curves 18–20, 26, 28, 42, 45, 53, 57–62, 64, 67, 69–70, 121, 138
cushions
  bird-shaped 18–20, 149
  fruity floor 72–6, 140
  true love 34–7, 158
cutting 10, 12, 32, 93, 117

de Castro Peake, Elisalex 46, 49
decorative stitches 100–4
Dixon, Jenny 12, 21
double-stitching 122
dresses
  toy 28
  trapeze sundress 46–52, 123, 128

easestitching 113
edgestitching 113
embellishments 141–3

embroidery 21–3
  free-motion machine 72, 75, 76, 80–2, 141–2
  transferring designs 18–20, 80, 83, 100
embroidery hoops 21–2, 100, 141–2
equipment 92–6

fabric 114–17
fabric feed 108
feed dog 108, 141
finishing off 97, 101
Fisher, Laura 60
flowers, fancy fabric 10–13, 150
free-arm 105
French knots 6, 64, 68–70, 104
French seams 46, 48, 50
fusible interfacing 38, 40
fusible webbing 72–5, 80–2, 143

gathers 53, 54, 135–6

hand stitching 6–13, 18–22, 24–33, 38–45, 58–60, 64–71, 77–83, 95, 97–104, 125
Hannah and Rosie 14, 17, 54
hemlines 48, 52, 124
hemming stitch 99
hems
  machine-stitched 14, 17, 46, 52, 84, 89, 124–7
  pressing 96
  types 124–9
herringbone stitch, blind 127
hot water bottle covers 77–9, 143
Hughes, Jane 32, 61

Jooles 40, 77–8

kimono top, tassel-fringed 14–17, 121, 134
knots 101
  away waste 101
  quick knotting 97

Larkins, Zoe 34, 37
leather 34–7, 116
lockstitch 108

machine-stitching 14–22, 24–9, 34–46, 52, 58–70, 72–89, 118–19, 124–7, 141–3

make-up brush roll 38–41
marking 93, 124, 146
measurements 84, 86, 92, 144–5
Moorby, Charlie 6, 9

Neale, Kirsty 66, 69, 71
needlecase, acorn leaf 42, 45
needles 95
New Craft House, The 17, 53
Nicolson, Clare 18, 20

patchwork quilt, easy peasy 30–3, 120, 139
patterns 144–5
peg bag, bird appliqué 21–3, 100, 102, 155
photo album cover 80–3, 153
pillow, badger 58–60, 151
pin cushions 42–4, 95
pinking 122
pinning 95, 118, 146
piping 140
  corded 72, 74, 75, 140
pleats, box 52
pockets 40–1, 57
presser feet 107, 109
pressing 30, 32, 77–8, 96
pyjama case, Dapper bear 64–8, 101, 130, 156

quilt 30–3, 120, 139

raw edges 122
ribbon 38–41, 62, 78
ruffles 40, 41
running stitch 10, 13, 18–20, 24, 28, 42, 45, 64, 67, 80, 83, 98

satin stitch 42, 44, 104
scissor keeper, acorn 42, 45
seam allowances 111
seams 118–23
  clipped 96
  curved 18–20, 26, 28, 42, 45, 58–62, 64, 67, 69–70, 121
  finishes 14, 16–17, 84, 87, 122
  flat 30, 32, 77–8, 96
  French 123
  grading 119
  intersecting 120
  machined 118–19
  plain straight 14, 16–17, 30, 32–3, 119

side 48, 50, 51
  trimming to neaten 18–20, 34, 69–70, 119
selvage 114
sewing darts 84, 87, 147
sewing machines 94, 105–13, 115, 124–7
sewing set, hedgehog 42–5
shrews in a shoe 24–9, 118, 154
skirt, button-up A-line 84–9, 132, 137, 147
sleep mask, foxy 69–71, 152
slipstitch 24, 28, 30, 33, 38, 41–2, 45, 58–60, 64, 67–70, 77–8, 80, 83, 98
stamping 38, 41
starting off 101, 110–12
straight stitch 38, 40, 53–4, 113
stretch stitch 54
stuffing shapes 9, 20, 28, 60

tacking 75, 95, 146
Tees, take three 52–7, 115, 138, 149
Thomas, Heather 72, 84, 88
thread 95, 101, 112
thread shanks 133
topstitching 24, 29–30, 32, 53, 57, 113, 126
trims 134–5
  fringe 14, 17, 53, 56, 134
  in-seam 34, 37, 61–2, 135
  lace 78
  peplum 54
  pom-pom 37
  tassel 56

utility stitches 97–9

velvet 77–8, 116

wadding 30, 32, 41, 45, 78
warp 114
wedding charms 6–9, 103, 148
weft 114
whipstitch 18–20, 42, 44, 98

yo-yo flowers 62
Youngs, Clare 26, 29

zigzag stitch 56, 62, 113, 122, 126, 132
zips 64, 67, 72, 75, 130–1

PUBLISHER'S ACKNOWLEDGEMENTS

This book would not have been possible without the input of all our fantastic crafty contributors. We would also like to thank Cheryl Brown, who has done a great job of pulling everything together and Sophie Yamamoto for her design work. Thanks to Kuo Kang Chen for his excellent illustrations, and Rachel Whiting and Rachael Smith for their photography. And of course, thanks must go to the fantastic team at Mollie Makes for all their help, in particular Cath Dean and Catherine Potter.

PHOTOGRAPHY CREDITS
Rachel Whiting: front cover and pp. 2, 5, 7, 11, 15, 19, 21, 23, 25, 27, 29, 31, 35, 37, 39, 45, 47, 50, 52, 53, 55, 56, 59, 60, 65, 68, 69, 71, 73, 76, 77, 79, 81, 85, 87 (top), 88 (bottom), 89 (bottom), 90, 91.

Rachael Smith: pp. 61, 62, 63.

For more information on *Mollie Makes* please visit molliemakes.com

Whatever the craft, we have the book for you – just head straight to Pavilion's crafty headquarters.

Pavilion Craft is the one-stop destination for all our fabulous craft books. Sign up for our regular newsletters and follow us on social media to receive updates on new books, competitions and interviews with our bestselling authors.

We look forward to meeting you!

www.pavilionbooks.com/craft

Published in the United Kingdom in 2020 by
Pavilion
43 Great Ormond Street
London
WC1N 3HZ

An imprint of Pavilion Books Company Ltd

Distributed in the United States and Canada by Sterling Publishing Co., Inc.
1166 Avenue of the Americas, New York, NY 10036

ISBN 978-1-91116-366-4

A CIP catalogue record for this book is available from the British Library.

10 9 8 7 6 5 4 3 2 1

Reproduction by Mission Productions Ltd, Hong Kong
Printed and bound by 1010 Printing International Ltd, China

www.pavilionbooks.com

FSC
MIX
Paper from responsible sources
FSC® C016973